HIGHdentity

HIGHdentity

Dr. John Powell

Scriptum Press, New York

HIGHdentity

ISBN: 978-0-9795213-9-3

Published by Scriptum Press, New York

Printed in the United States of America

Dedication

I dedicate this book to our three wonderful children: Jennifer Brantley, Jake Powell and Josh Powell. As well as their mates, Stacy Brantley, April Powell and Lisa Powell who are such a great addition to our family.

This dedication includes their awesome children, our grandchildren: Hannah Marie Brantley, Wade Brantley and Stella Rae Brantley. Plus, Allie and Jacob Powell and newest of all, 3 month old, Joseph Wilson Powell.

We are all a big expanded family. They love us all and we all love them. They are a special blessing to all of us grandparents. I am just one among many. God has blessed our family. And we want to bless Him back!

TABLE OF CONTENTS

1 Get Under the Shadow of the Most High God   14

2 We Are More than Conquerors   18

3 Overcomers   22

4 HIGHdentity versus Low Esteem   24

5 The Curse is Reversed   26

6 Chosen   28

7 Human Nature Out of Control   30

8 Lust versus Love   32

9 Surface Joy versus Deep Joy   34

10 Strife versus Peace   36

11 What None of Us Have: Patience   38

12 Overcoming Weaknesses of the Flesh   40

13 Realize Your True HIGHdentity   42

14 Forgiven   44

15 Salvation is Created   46

16 The Way to Go   48

17 Touchable, Tested, Thorough and Trustworthy   53

18 Jesus is Sacred   55

19 He is Enough, Exclusive and Fulfilling   57

20 Challenging - Creative - Meaningful   59

21 Salvation Work Out   60

22 Be Transformed   64

23 Can Do People   68

24 Broken   70

25 Blessed With Every Spiritual Blessing   73

26 Delivered to Stand   76

27 Eternal Purpose   81

28 Adjust to God's Viewpoint   85

29 Begin New Now   88

30 Bring Every Thought Captive   91

31 De-gripping the Grasshopper Mentality 93

32 Get Out of the Hole 96

33 Something to Look Forward To 99

34 Don't Let Anyone Blow You Out 103

35 Know God Better Than Your Favorite TV Show 107

36 When You Are Down and Out 110

37 Sit -- Walk – Stand 113

38 Stay Connected 116

39 Spiritual Starvation 118

40 Confess to Possess 120

41 God Uses a Restless Man or Woman 122

42 Let the Spirit of God Produce Good Fruit in Us 127

43 Till We All Come to Maturity in Christ Jesus 129

44 Be Content with God 132

45 Connect and Continue 134

46 Marching to Zion 138

47 Love Sharpens Love 140

48 Afraid We Will Turn Them Off 143

49 How Far Are We Going to Go With Jesus? 145

50 The Power of Agreeing 147

51 Sniffing versus Tasting 150

52 Awesome Reverence 153

53 Back to the Bible 155

54 I Anticipate My Mate 160

55 Get a Grip on Our Great God 166

56 Pardon Me Boys! Is This the Ice Cream Truck to
Wal-mart? 169

57 Self-help Winds Down to Zero 171

58 Take the Spurs Off 173

59 Repent Quickly 175

60 Is This the Slim-Fast Bus to the Gym? 177

61 Jesus Come 179

PREFACE

This book was written out of the struggle I had going through a change in family and ministry in the early 1990's.

My Dad had always wanted me to just be somebody. It would probably shock him, yet encourage him, to know that I found my true HIGHdentity in a Christian Therapy Unit in Van Nuys, California. HIGHdentity, found in the title of this book is a concept developed by me, years ago.

Many people set out in life to "Find themselves." Many times it means finding the right mate, the right job and the right direction in life. I have enjoyed all of my years. But the rough times I went through in the 90's and 2000's really helped me "Let Christ be formed in me." That is my prayer for all of us. To let the Lord of Life be formed in us more and more, for He alone is able to keep us from falling into mediocrity and conformity. He alone can elevate us to being our best selves, to reaching our HIGHdentity in Him. Thanks be to God, Who always causes us to triumph in Jesus Christ, The Champion Over Evil.

The Galilean Peasant

Well, let me tell you the story of the Galilean peasant

who was born in a stable bare…
He reached all of creation with a new dimension.
People said, "Here's a man who is rare."
But did He ever give up, No! He never gave up.
As pure love He spread all around --
He put life into rhythm and He made it higher -- He said,
"Turn, start all over again."
One day Jesus met the woman at the well and He said,

"Woman don't you know it's true? That this well
running water only hits the surface, and can never really
satisfy you!"

He walked the country, crossing hill and valley
reaching men who were lost in sin. He gave hope to the
hopeless and He reached the masses saying, "Turn! You
must begin it again."

Now you who are searching for a deeper meaning
Seeking life so abundantly…
Choose Jesus as your leader, and He'll make your life completer….
Come to Him, and He'll set you free!

The above words are to a song I wrote in the 1960's,
doing youth ministry. The song is to the tune of the
Kingston Trio's, MTA (the story about a man named Charlie
who got lost on the Massachusetts Transit Authority Train).

INTRODUCTION

HIGHdentity is a concept I developed working through a very rough time in my life. I know what it feels to be rejected, and on top of that, changing jobs, opening a new bookstore, losing money big time, going into debt and fighting negative thoughts of failure like in a war. After three years of fighting for my sanity, I went for help.

I drove to Fairfax, Virginia for counseling, but that was not thorough enough for my condition. Then I went to North Carolina to a recovery farm and the leader told me to go spend two or three hours alone with God. That was the last thing I wanted to hear. I wanted help in how to have peace and how to stop battling negative thoughts all the time. Losing my wife of 21 years was bad enough, but losing in a business that I thought would do well, and now thinking I could lose my mind was just too much. Whew! I was at the bottom crying out for help.

Next, I called 1-800-Help-4-me, which is Dr. Fred Gross Christian Therapy and after talking to the counselor on the phone for forty-five minutes, I was relieved that someone understood what I was facing. The Therapy Group flew me out to Van Nuys, Ca, and when I got there, I sat down and cried for about an hour. Actually, I felt relieved to find the depth of help I needed.

At last, the road to recovery began for me. The best and most effective part was the Scripture Therapy with a young man named David. We had an hour session each evening. He told me I was "Not a failure, but more than a conqueror through Jesus our Lord." I would respond and tell him the same. I knew Romans 8:37, the place that verse comes from, had even preached it in my twenty-five years of ministry in the Methodist church. Applying it to my losing situation, and overcoming the barrage of negative bullets the enemy threw at me, was a new experience.

It worked! After twenty-six days of Scripture Therapy, I got it. It was deep in my spirit. Way down past all the damaged emotions and awful thoughts. It wasn't just the "failure and rejection" thoughts. I had so many sad thoughts, of losing the unity of our family. I was really in a battleground. And when we are going through the battle for our sanity and self-worth, we need people, people who know how to encourage us with truth, and not just pad our pain with medications and isolation.

The need to ventilate is also a must. When we bury our anger and hurt, we store up negative energy that will explode later. We don't need to explode it on anyone, especially someone we love. No wonder the Bible warns us to 'Not let the sun go down on our anger.' Anger can eat a hole in us, and those we let it out on. As my wonderful counselor so wisely said, "It's not what you're eating; it's what's eating you." How true it is.

I kept burying my pain and hurt and covering it up with hard work and staying busy trying to get three lovely children through college and through the threshold of life. Buried anger can lead to depression. I was diagnosed as being "clinically depressed," by my counselor on the phone. But I would never agree with the many thoughts I had that tried to tell me, "I am so depressed." I had read the book, "What you say is what you get!" I knew not to agree with the negative, so I didn't. I kept fighting back.

By fighting back, I mean, every time I had the thought that I was depressed, I said out loud, "No, I'm not. I am impressed with Jesus Christ!" And that would combat anything the enemy could throw my way. How blessed I was to have read that book on not saying what you feel when it is negative. How true. And it works. I never gave up. I kept digging into God's word and finding out from the Father of All Creation who I was, and am.

1

GET UNDER THE SHADOW OF THE MOST HIGH GOD

The very first thing I learned is that we are not failures just because we lose our mates or jobs or money or sense of accomplishment. We are who God says we are. We can stand on that through hell and high water, because Jesus defeated the devil in the wilderness of temptation, when the enemy tried to get the Savior of mankind to put the physical ahead of the spiritual, by turning the stones into bread. That was after forty days of fasting, and excruciating hunger.

But Jesus refused. He stood His ground with, "Man shall not live by bread alone, but by every Word that comes from God." That is good strategy! What if we eat the most delicate food down here on earth and miss The Bread of Life. Jesus is The Bread of life. Depriving ourselves of so much food will help us get a grip on His superior value.

Putting the physical first is thinking we are failures when we lose our jobs or money or accomplishments. There is much more to life than what we have. It's more about who we are. God defines that very clearly for us in His word. We just have to dig it out and live by it. Jesus, the master model of God on earth, lived primarily by every word of God. He believed it to the point of praying in the garden, "Not my will but Thine be done." Now that's standing on the word, and obeying the Father in the highest.

The second temptation to failure is to take unnecessary risks. Jesus refused to jump off the pinnacle of the Temple, for He would never use God's power for Himself. He would never show off, or take unnecessary risks. He said, "We shall not tempt the Lord our God!" 1 Corinthians 6:12 says the same thing. 'As Christians we are free to do whatever we want. But we are not to take unnecessary risks, or do anything that might enslave us.' That means anything that might get such a grip on us we can't stop it even if we wanted to.

An ounce of prevention is worth a pound of cure. So many times we just plunge into the deep waters of unnecessary risk, and take the first drink, thinking we can control it. That's pride and pride goes before a fall. How many teenagers had sexual intercourse for the first time and backed off from it? Probably none. The flesh is weak and profits nothing. That's the wisdom of God, coming through the mouth of Jesus the Son of God.

There's another basic temptation to failure that Jesus faced, and we all face: bowing to evil. Jesus refused to take the whole world from the devil by bowing to him. How stupid to bow to a fallen angel. Yet we bow to him and the world, and he is lord of this world. Jesus is Lord of the kingdom of God, which is within us. We can go either way, but Christ reminds us that we "Cannot serve God and this world." We live in the world, but are not to be conformed to it and its lust for more things and its use of people to get things.

We are not failures. God believes in us, even "While we were yet sinners." Jesus said, "He who sins is a slave to sin." He is The Son of God and only He can set us free, free from the penalty for sin, which is death. He paid that for us. And free from the power of sin, which is being entrapped to the sinful desires gratified in this world.

We are also failures if we agree with our feelings and negative thoughts and don't get up out of the quagmire of low self-esteem. The way out is to believe we are who God says we are. Yes, even while we are down under the circumstances of life. We have to begin to see ourselves in a new light, the light of the Father and the Son, who is The Light of The World.

Here's the way I got it. I read Psalm 91 and agreed that I was "Under the shadow of The Most High God." I didn't feel like it, or look like it, and my circumstances certainly didn't match it, but I believed what God said, not what my feelings said, or the enemy of my soul echoed in my thoughts. I began to see myself as, "Under the Shadow of The Most High God." Not under the circumstances.

You can do the very same thing. No matter what your circumstances, don't get under them. See yourself under the Most High God. He will bring you through your trouble. He says so. "Many are the afflictions of the righteous, but the Lord delivers us from them all." That really is thorough deliverance. Thanks be to God! Praise the name of Jesus. You can make it. Just as I did. It is not us; it is Christ in us -- our hope of glory. Our hope of glory starts right where we are, bogged down in the pitfalls of life. What we do, when we don't know what to do? We stand on the promises. The gates of hell shall not prevail against us because all the demons in the world cannot hold back the truth of God from setting us free. Jesus took the offensive for us to set us free. When the Son of God sets us free, we are free indeed. Praise God! Thank you, Jesus!

2

WE ARE MORE THAN CONQUERORS

Through Jesus Christ our Lord, we can win with Him, because He is for us, even when we are losing in this world. That's the power of always triumphing in Christ our Lord. The victory is already won. God is inviting us to come participate and celebrate with Him. Jesus overcame sin, distance from God, death, judgment and hell.....and low self-esteem. He brought on HIGHdentity, which is Christ-esteem, as opposed to self-esteem.

The victory over low-self esteem, feelings of no worth, being down and depressed is near to us in Christ Jesus for He has already won the victory. He says, "In the world you will have tribulation. But be of good cheer. I have overcome the world." Now that is a comprehensive and important statement of truth to make. Jesus overcame all the temptations we face to find our identity in the world, and all it offers us. He found His HIGHdentity in His Father. He refused to bow to the allurements of this world for gratification and esteem.

We can do the same, by realizing who we are in Him.

He has chosen us. God has predestined us to be conformed to His image, not the world's image. We must learn to be content with who we are in Him, and not try to find ourselves out there in the mad scramble for success in the world. It's just not there. What if we gained the whole world and lost our own souls, what would that profit us? Absolutely nothing.

We are to seek higher values in the Lord. They are found in the fruit of the Spirit of God working in us to bring forth love, joy, peace, patience, kindness, goodness, faithfulness, gentleness and self-control. Those are the values directly from the Father that cannot be found or bought on earth. In addition, He freely gives us His Spirit to guide us into them, and all truth. Jesus said, "Receive the Holy Spirit." What a gift. What a presence. What power to produce the qualities we seek in the wrong places in the world.

We must see ourselves as more than conquerors, not as worthless and failures. We get the eternal benefits of Jesus conquering the temptation to find life in the world. He found purpose in doing God's Will and in spending quality time with The Father. We can, also. We can then find the power from Him to conquer the ever nagging ache of low self-esteem and not being good enough.

Jesus' death on the cross for us means we are of eternal value to God the Father. It also gives meaning to a meaningless existence here on earth without some over-arching purpose in life. We are valuable because He paid the price for us that money can't buy. He purchased our eternal salvation. He literally bought us back to God, even though we sin and stray away. That gives us eternal purpose, in this life and in the life to come. God wants us.

He had rather die than live without us. He proved it through the sacrifice of Jesus for us.

Now we can get the vision of being more than a conqueror through the Lord and His eternal love for us. We are born to lose, but born again to win! Who in his or her right mind had rather have the riches of this world rather than eternal fellowship with God? Jesus wants us to choose Him first. Seeking Him first lets Him know we want Him as much as He wants us. It's a two way street. He pours out His love for us. We pour out our love for Him.

We can conquer fear because of who we are in Christ. For God has not given us a spirit of fear, but of power love and a sound mind. Jesus often said, "Fear not!" There is nothing that can intimidate us as we walk in the light of God's Word. Every obstacle can be overcome by the people of God who are more than Conquerors! Because we know that the battle for significance is already won. Jesus won it for us on the cross. And God declares it in His Word, which is forever settled in Heaven.

That's exactly what I am writing about. How I found out that I was eternally significant to God, though someone I loved hurt me deeply with rejection. God is much more important than any person on this earth. Even though someone close to us rejects us, we can find great worth in our Father. It's called, Christ-esteem; not self-esteem. Self-esteem is so limited and eventually worthless. But God is going to love us no matter what happens. People will fail us and reject us and give up on us. Thank God because He never gives up on us.

See yourself as more than a conqueror through the love of God in Christ Jesus, and you will be able to conquer anything that hinders you, anything that holds you back from following God, anything that controls you in a negative way. God is able, to keep us from falling, even after we have already fallen many times. You can begin today to start realizing your potential in Christ Jesus. Just meditate on being more than a conqueror, and believe it. Believe God. Trust Him when He says you can do all things through Him who strengthens you. He is able. He is God. He is The Mighty Conqueror! He came that we might have life more abundant, which includes being more than a conqueror. Amen! And Praise The Lord.

3

OVERCOMERS

We are overcomers in this life. Even though we have been overcome by bad habits and sins of the flesh, though we have failed at many things, and though we may be addicted to whatever, we can still realize our potential as overcomers. Jesus said, "Bless is he who overcomes. He shall be given a crown of life."

The Lord knows we are going to sin and fail and drift far away from Him and lose our purpose and meaning and significance in life. That's why He sent The Savior of all mankind. Not only did He pay the penalty for our sins, He also set the perfect example for what we can be, in Him. He looks at us as 'new creations.' New, because 'He that the Son sets free is free indeed' this means being free from the past. We are to forget it. And press on to the prize of the high calling of God in Christ Jesus. We can do it from any point of failure in life. We can't get too bad for God. Good overcomes bad.

Jesus knew who He was. He said very explicitly, "I am The Way." He was not confused about His identity with

The Father in Heaven, who sent Him to rescue us from being lost. As long as we follow Him, we will never be lost again. Never! All we have to do is follow the light. Jesus is The Light of The World. Let's stay out of the darkness. Yet, His light shines even in the dark. It shows us the way out.

Jesus said, "I am the truth." This overshadows any errors and arrows of lies shot at us by the devil. Satan comes to kill, steal and destroy. Jesus came that we might have life more abundant. That comes from knowing the truth, for the truth will set us free, free to walk in the light of His words, which are spirit and life. Free to detect error and resist it by turning away from it and following the truth, Jesus Himself. Praise God. The truth of all eternity is a person, the person who loves us enough to die for us, and give us His resurrection power.

Jesus is the Life. Actually, He is the Resurrection and the Life. That is so powerful. It is what we are so desperate for. We are a walking corpse of human flesh, with no permanent life in us because we cut ourselves off from God's life when we sin. Jesus re-connects us to The Source of All Life, God the Father. Now we have eternal life flowing in us, as we receive Jesus as our Lord and Savior. Eternal life is in knowing God, through His Son. It gives us the power to become overcomers. We can overcome our weak flesh, the world and the devil. Praise God.

4

HIGHdentity VERSUS LOW SELF-ESTEEM

HIGHdentity is based on who we are In Christ Jesus, which is eternal fact. Self-esteem is based on what we do for a living, how much we make on our jobs, how big our banking accounts are, and what our accomplishments are. All of these can dwindle or be totally wiped out. We can lose our jobs, get a cut in pay, not have any money in savings, or not enough in our monthly expense account. Plus, what we have accomplished in building up experience in a certain job may be lost, due to a change in work.

Who we are in Christ Jesus is here to stay. It is written in The Word of God, which is forever settled in Heaven. It's our personal identity, which I call, HIGHdentity. It is much higher than any self-worth we can find here on earth. It is our status in the family of God. And it is given to us by God our Father, through Jesus Christ His Son. We can't earn it; we can just receive it as a gift.

It's not about self, as in selfish. This is where sin starts. It has nothing to do with pride. It comes when we are humble enough, or desperate enough, to seek it out for ourselves. Nobody can give it to us. We have to want it bad enough to go for it. He or she who seeks God - and who are in Him, will find Him with all His eternal benefits included.

That's exactly what I did. I sought my identity in the Lord, and I found more than I could even find in a job, vocation, an accomplishment, or the things money can buy here on earth. I found that we are 'somebody' to God -- somebody He will lift us up out of the pit of low self-esteem, and elevate to where we are, sitting with Christ Jesus in heavenly places." Now that's really moving up. It is equally available to all who care enough, and look in the right direction, to find this HIGHdentity.

Our true identity is found in Christ, not in human accomplishment. Jesus accomplished more on the cross than we could all together accomplish on this earth. He ransomed the human race from sin and death. He bought us back from the slavery of a fallen angel, Satan. He frees us to be our best selves in Him. He gives us power over our past through forgiveness and power to live a righteous life through His Holy Spirit.

5

THE CURSE IS REVERSED

He did it! Jesus came to earth and did what no other man in all of history could possibly do. He reversed the curse hanging over the whole human race. We were cursed because we sin. Now we are forgiven because through Jesus, God forgives us, not just for sins, but for being sinners. We become Saints, only by the grace of our Savior, for 'He became sin for us, that we, the sinner, might become the righteousness of God, In Him."

The curse meant we could not do anything eternally productive, as we only could operate in our weak flesh, which is weak and profits nothing. Nothing! Our lives were in vain until Jesus came and turned our spiritual barrenness into born-of-God productivity. Not only did Jesus free us from the guilt and shame of our past sins, He restores us to our connection as authentic children of God by sending His Holy Spirit into our hearts and lives He does this so we can be born again and live productive lives.

We can now press on to the prize of the high calling of God in Christ Jesus. We can know God personally and receive His Spirit into our lives to quicken us spiritually and give us the capacity to walk with God, and not continue to sin and have to run or hide from Him, as Adam and Eve did.

We can grow in grace and the knowledge of God. We march to the tune of the Master Designer who has redeemed us from the dead end of sin. We are righteous through Jesus' shed, pure blood for us. Now, we can begin to life clean and free from sin. If we sin, God is faithful and just, to forgive us of our sin, and cleanse us from all unrighteousness.

Jesus is able, to keep us from falling, and present us faultless before His presence with exceedingly great joy. What a blessing. He gives us a new status with God and a new start in completing our lives here on earth. Christ Jesus forever connected time and eternity. He bridged the gap between us and God, and connects us with righteous living. We are free from our old patterns of sin and self-indulgence. We are free to be the best that God intended us to be which brings great joy to our souls. He has made us whole, both now and for all eternity. Praise be to the Father, and the Son, and the Holy Spirit.

6

CHOSEN

We are chosen by God, through Jesus, to become His own special people. A chosen generation, called out of darkness into His marvelous light to be Ambassadors for Christ. Called to continue the work of the ministry that Jesus started and is finishing from heaven through us. He gives us the keys to the kingdom of God. Whatever we bind (restrict), will be bound. Whatever we loose (set free), will be free!

We are chosen to the royal priesthood. We are to stand in the gap for the lost. To intercede for hurting people even when they don't realize it. Jesus ever lives in Heaven to intercede for us. We line up with Him and will not give God rest until He makes Jerusalem and Israel His chosen people and the church, The Body of Christ, a praise in this earth. We go into labor for souls to be saved, and for nations to be turned to God. This nation needs to return to the principles of the bible which George Washington said it could not function without.

We are somebody to God. When we have Christ in

us, we have everything. That is, everything of eternal significance. Even though we miss many opportunities to excel on this earth, we can excel with God. And start right where we are, in the pitfalls of life, struggling with negative thought attacks, feeling low, and experiencing turbulence in our circumstances. I did. I thought I was going to lose before I re-established my connection with God. I learned to live as a chosen person, not rejected. God will never leave or reject us, though people do.

Jesus said, "I chose you, to go and bear much fruit." Good fruit is not determined by our past, or even our personal performance. It is determined by the Spirit of God moving in us to produce good fruit of love, joy, peace, patience, kindness, goodness, faithfulness, gentleness and self-control. Those high qualities are possible for anyone who follows Jesus and continues living by His word, not by feelings.

We walk by faith, not sight. Our faith must be in God's holy word. We can make it, but God requires faith. We can do it, because we are following a victorious Savior, and a good God who will not withhold any good thing from we who love Him, and follow Him, by faith. Above all, take up the shield of faith. It will get you through the battleground of life, in the low places.

7

HUMAN NATURE OUT OF CONTROL

The root problem we all have is that we sin. Jesus pointed out that when we sin, we are the slaves of sin. All sin is enslaving. We desperately need freedom from the tendency, the temptation and the environment of sin. So the Lord gives us a new nature, His, The Holy Spirit, to give us the power over sin. We overcome our weak flesh by the power of His Spirit working in us to convict us and lead us into righteousness, not sin.

Inevitably, we still have to choose. He just gives us a new alternative, the alternative not to sin. It's our new choice now. We must first exercise our will and choose God's way, not the way of the human flesh, the world and the devil. Without the Lord in our lives, we have no choice. We sin, and we are controlled by sin. The good news is that 'he that the Son sets free is free indeed.' No more chains, He bought our liberty. The truth has triumphed in victory. He that the Son sets free need not be enslaved anymore. We are no longer bound.

Then we have to deal with the environment of sin.

We stay around sinners and we sin. We walk with the wise who don't sin, and we are more likely to not choose to sin. Our peers are very influential on us. So we have to be careful who we hang around. If we are around positive people who love the Lord and walk by faith, we will be encouraged. And we can encourage them. It's a reciprocal influence. Encouragement builds encouragement.

Self-control is a fruit of the Holy Spirit. We don't have it in ourselves to control ourselves. Paul the Apostle made it clear that we do the very things we don't want to do. In other words, we don't do the things we wish to do. We are caught up in the vicious cycle of sin and death. Who will free us? Thanks be to God through our Lord Jesus Christ. He is the Son and is not bound to anything. He can set the slaves, us, free. Praise Him!

8

LUST VERSUS LOVE

Our human natures are in a battle constantly between the flesh and the spirit. Part of it is lust battling love. God wants us to love. Our flesh desires to get from someone, and not give, as does love. The problem with lust is that it is never satisfied. We can never get enough to satisfy the lust of our eyes, the lust of the flesh or the pride of life. Lust is selfish. It thinks of its own gratification. It takes, and doesn't give.

Love is of God, for God is love. It gives like a thoughtless prodigal, and trembles, lest it has done too little. That's the kind of love Jesus has for us. He gave all of Himself on the cross, in addition to giving of His time and energy on earth to heal and direct and lead people in 'the way.' We have to learn to follow His example and love people. Take the initiative in reaching out to them. Do something good for them first. Then, love sharpens love.

Another problem with lust is that it operates on the law of diminishing returns. It takes more and more of sex or alcohol or sweets or whatever fills our desires at the time.

We are never filled. We are left empty, frustrated and mocked by the allure of lust.

Love does not mock us. It operates on the law of increasing returns. It fills our deepest longings. It satisfies our very souls. For we were made for love, by God who is love. And we will never be satisfied until we receive His love and allow Him to fill us with His loving kindness, which is better than life. Then we are content, for Love fulfills the law. Lust never could.

9

SURFACE JOY VERSUS DEEP JOY

Our relationship with God through Christ brings us a deep joy that reaches to the depths of our being. The Joy of The Lord is our strength. When we have His Joy, we are strong. That's what it means to be strong in The Lord. Plus, Jesus gives us a joy that the world cannot give us, and cannot take away. It stems from the peace He gives that gives us rest and security.

The fun we have in the world from just pleasure, only tickles the surface of our satisfaction. It is so shallow. It can never reach our real need for joy. The world can make us happy. But that is based on chance. The Lord gives us joy, which is based on covenant. We are in covenant with The Author of Joy. Jesus got joy from going to the cross even, because what greater joy can a person have than to win our souls back to God for eternity, and change our eternal destiny.

We can share the joy the Lord gives us by reaching out to those in need. To see them hear the gospel of love, joy and peace and come to believe in Jesus Christ as their Savior is the highest joy. Heaven rejoices when one soul is saved. We can rejoice, too, for we can be ambassadors for Christ, and lead lost people to the Lord and eternal life.

10

STRIFE VERSUS PEACE

Human nature strives against itself and against God and others. In our raw state, we get into conflict with others over small matters, usually, things which really don't matter. It's because we think in our selfishness, we must have our own way, and that is not good. We argue and fight for 'our way,' causing us to lose friends. Nobody wants to be around a selfish person. Selfish people isolate themselves.

Next, there is striving with our maker. Woe to the person who strives with his or her maker. God does not permit rebellion, for rebellion is as the sin of witchcraft. God expects and demands humility. We must humble ourselves before the mighty hand of God. In due time, He will exalt us. We are not supposed to exalt ourselves. That's pride, and pride comes before a fall.

The reason we strive with others and God is that we strive within ourselves. Our selfish nature wants to control us. When we give in to its selfish desires we lose. We lose God and other people. We are pre-destined to be conformed to the image of Jesus, who was totally unselfish. We must crucify our selfish desires, put God first and others before ourselves. It works. We will be at peace with ourselves and others and God. It is worth the effort to be unselfish.

11

WHAT NONE OF US HAVE: PATIENCE

Endurance, patience and self-control, by the Spirit of God, are the high virtues The Lord wants to build in us. The difficult part is that we learn patience in very impatient situations, such as waiting on a red light without fuming with frustration, standing in line without losing our cool, or waiting on someone who is late, without coming unglued. Such things put us on the edge of patience, if we wait for it to be developed in our daily situations.

Jesus endured such hardship against sinners, to the point of shedding His own perfect blood. We will never be tested that far. The things we face are weak compared to what He went through. The key is to learn to endure the small tests of our patience, then we can face the larger ones, like having to retake an exam, or waiting to be married, or waiting till we are sixteen to drive a car, with license.

The following is a song I wrote doing prison ministry back in the 90's. It is to the tune of Credence Clearwater Revival's, Midnight Special. It is called, "Midnight Savior."

Let the midnight Savior
Shine His Light on you
He made it through Calvary
And He can pull you through.
Whatever you're facing
Lift your head up high
Cause the Midnight Savior
He won't let you die!

We can make it through the pitfalls of life, if we keep our eyes on Jesus, The Author and Finisher of our Faith. He made it through the rejection and crucifixion of men on earth. We can make it through what seems to be heavy trials, but what are small compared to what He went through. God brings us to something, to bring us through it. He can, and He will. He is able to keep us from falling.

12

OVERCOMING WEAKNESSES OF THE FLESH

Our human flesh has many weaknesses, like the impatience I just mentioned in the last chapter; but there is more. Being rude is one of the characteristics of weak human nature. Our selves venting their full wrath can be rather rude. We need the kindness of the Spirit operating in us, else, we are rude. Kindness is stronger than rudeness. It is a choice we must make to stay in close relationships.

'Bad to the bone,' is one of the weak traits of us humans. Sin has corrupted us to the point of needing to be saved. Our hearts are "Desperately wicked," according to Jeremiah. We can be just as bad as we wish. The worst of the bad is rejecting Jesus Christ, especially by just ignoring Him. We are on the way to hell without Him. To think we don't need Him is bad.

Only the Lord can turn our badness into goodness. We just have to repent and turn to Him and admit we need help, desperately, and trust Him to change us into good people. We can be just as good as we are willing to follow the example of Jesus, our perfect Savior, who believes we can change.

I heard a counselor say that we don't change much after marriage. I say, "We had better!" We are following a perfect Savior. That means constant big time change. Plus, we are living with another imperfect human being, and that means lots of changes and adjustments both ways. Or we separate ourselves.

Human nature can be abrasive. The loving Spirit of God smoothes off our rough edges so that we are gentle. That is a needed quality coming only from the Lord. We need it since we are called by God to live in peace and to be cooperative. We are not grind on people's nerves, over-react or get into a tizzy of emotional upheaval. We are to take it easy. We can do it when we walk in obedience to the Lord Jesus!

13

REALIZE YOUR TRUE HIGHdentity

To realize our true HIGHdentity in Christ Jesus, we must learn to see ourselves as ,"Under the shadow of the Most High God," as in Psalm 91. Otherwise, we are victims of our circumstances, our negative thoughts and low feelings. When we get the vision of being under the guidance and security of our loving Heavenly Father, regardless of our trials, we can rise above the negative and walk in the positive with God.

God is a "Very present help in time of trouble," Psalm 46. We need to see Him that way, especially when we are under the attack of negative thoughts and walking through the wilderness of our lives when we feel lost and afraid. God helps us get rid of all fear. Jesus said, "Fear not," many times. Perfect love casts out fear. And God and Jesus are perfect love. Get under their umbrella of truth.

God is our 'exceeding joy!' We need His joy for deep, inner strength. The lack of joy equals no strength. With His strength, we can do all things through Christ who strengthens us. It's a plus from operating under His shadow of guidance. He will lead us into all truth. For Jesus is The Truth. We will never be lost following Him.

God is a rewarder, of we who diligently seek Him. The Lord challenges us to, "Follow me," Jesus said. That means pressing on to the prize of the high calling of God in Christ Jesus. It means to lay aside every weight, and the sin that so easily besets us, and to keep our eyes on Jesus. He knows how to get to the finish line, heaven. He's already there, sitting at the right hand of Almighty God.

Jesus ever lives to make intercession for us. We just need to seek Him with all our hearts. He wants to get us to where He is, now and then. Now, in the sense of "Letting Christ be formed in us." Then, in the sense of, "I go to prepare a place for you, that where I am, you may be also." That is taking care of our immediate needs and our eternal needs. What else could we possibly need?

14

FORGIVEN

God was in Christ, reconciling the world unto Himself. That means we are forgiven, not just of our sins, but for being sinners. It's in our blood, our environment and choices. We are responsible for our own lives before God. But He, knowing our deepest need, sent Jesus to reconcile us to Himself by forgiving us for being imperfect, and getting us started on the road to perfection.

We are not perfect in behavior however we can be perfect in following Jesus. When we sin, we confess and He forgives us and cleanses us from all unrighteousness. God expects us to get better. Christ Jesus is being formed in us by the power of His strong spirit. We can overcome sin. We can be like the Lord. He deserves us. He bought us with a price: the blood of Jesus.

The closer we get to God, by spending time with Him, the closer we get to being like Him. Yet, we are still in the flesh, and we must train our flesh to follow the Spirit. We must wean our very souls from this world, and all its allurements. We can do it for we are more than conquerors through Jesus.

It is easy to become Holy, when we "Set the Lord always before us! Because He is at our right hand we shall not be moved." Psalm 16.8. Plus, when we "taste and see that the Lord is good," we won't settle for eating with the pigs on the lusts of this world.

God is good! All things work for good for those of us who follow Him and His purpose. How good of God to forgive us for being imperfect! What motivation to give up sinning. The love of Jesus Christ constrains us to follow Him. He loves us more than anyone ever did or could, therefore let us keep our eyes on Jesus.

Because we are forgiven by God, we can forgive other people when they hurt us. That is a must, not a choice. God requires us to forgive, or He won't forgive us for not forgiving. Some people say they just can't forgive others who hurt them so badly. I say we can, if we quit trying to do it out of hurt feelings, and do it out of obedience to God. We will feel better.

15

SALVATION IS CREATED

When Jesus died on the cross, our salvation was created. God does not hold our trespasses against us. Human nature is like a 'wild olive branch,' but God chose to save us anyway. One of the greatest lifts in realizing our HIGHdentity in Christ is that we are 'saved' by grace, the undeserved mercy and grace of God. Not of good works, lest anyone boast. It's all God's doing, to the extreme of sacrificing His Son Jesus on the cross.

We are saved from the wrath of God against sin. God doesn't hate us. He hates sin, and what it does to us. It separates us from our best selves, healthy relationships with others and from God. On the other hand, salvation brings us close to God, and into real intimacy of the spirit. That is where intimacy is. Not in the flesh or in human relationships. It is in our personal relationship with God our Father. It's being closer than close.

We certainly need that kind of closeness in our relationships with our families and others. We get so offended and put out when someone does something we don't like. But God keeps us close through love and forgiveness and continuously reaching out to be in good fellowship with others, especially those who hurt us, or try to control us.

We are saved from the penalty and power of sin. Jesus' blood forever changes our status with God to "Not condemned." There is no condemnation for those who are in Christ Jesus, who walk not according to the flesh, but according to the spirit. We are free from judgment, even by a Holy God.

We are saved from the power of sin. We have a new alternative. We can choose not to sin. We can follow righteousness and reject sin as we grow in grace and the knowledge of our Lord and Savior. We can improve drastically. We can overcome any sin that has a grip on us. We are completely delivered from evil. We have the potential to be like Jesus. Praise God!

16

THE WAY TO GO

The way to go is through Jesus Christ. There was nothing attractive about Him physically or worldly. He had nothing this world considers important. He was who He was, and that remains totally attractive. He is the same, yesterday, today and forever. Such quality no person can match. Everyone else who has graced this planet dies. Jesus experienced an earthly death, but is still living, with God in heaven. Every knee will bow to Him and every tongue confess, that He is Lord, to the glory of God the Father.

He was the most passionate man who ever lived. He had extreme mercy on the masses, went around doing good, healing all who were oppressed by the devil. The devil tries to get us to think we are failures. Jesus ensures us we are worth dying for, and worth restoring to His image so we can live victorious lives here on earth. He is passionate for us. God the Father is not willing for even one of us to perish. He deserves that we get passionate about Him -- to get up off our fatty acids and get it in gear -- to seek Him with all our hearts -- to go after Him like a deer, famished in the desert, being chased by dogs, longing for a drink of water. God has moved dynamically in our direction. He expects us to move back toward Him. He will not accept lukewarmness. That is out. Following Him in full faith is in.

Jesus is irresistible. He has the words of eternal life. Where else can we go? Why settle for temporary, worldly existence, only scratching the surface, when we can have life more abundant. Jesus said, "My words are spirit and life." His words are more important than riches, fame or popularity. We are to live by every word of God, just as Jesus certainly did. Then we can walk in the right direction, pursuing God and experiencing eternal life. For eternal life begins when we receive the gift of salvation, and begin to work out our own salvation with fear and trembling, lest we fall short of doing God's will.

Jesus is inspiring. He sacrificed His perfect life for us, while we were yet sinners. That supreme act of love will motivate us to follow Him. Love inspires love. Love is the springboard for our actions, not selfishness. Love is sacrifice. Doing things for others they don't deserve, or expect. It will bring on a response of gratitude that will change people for good forever. As in the movie, *Fireproof!,* when the husband paid big bucks for his wife's Mother's medical equipment, it really saved their marriage. She originally thought a flirting doctor paid for it, when, in fact, he had only paid a small portion. When she found out the truth, it set her free to be committed to her husband, and be restored in a relationship with him. He found the Lord, through a forty day venture of commitment and faith. She made it clear that she wanted what he had, because it made him sacrifice for her. Sacrifice will spark any cold relationship, especially in marriage.

The Lord Jesus is courageous. He steadfastly set His face to go to Jerusalem, knowing that there He would be crucified. He went anyway. He came to seek and save the lost, including all of us. In order to save us, He had to be courageous enough to die for our sins. He prayed in the Garden of Gethsemane, "Not my will but Thine be done." He prayed that through sweat drops of blood. Nobody wants to die, certainly not on a cross as He did. He did it with forgiveness on his lips.

Not in vain! Jesus life was not in vain. He committed His Spirit back into the hands of God Almighty, in His last few seconds on the cross. God raised Him from the dead! Jesus is The Resurrection and The Life! The same power that raised Him from the dead is available to raise us up from the deadness of sin and despair and depression and divorce, debt, loneliness, fear and anything else that keeps us down. Jesus says to us, "Receive the Holy Spirit," which is the power to overcome anything that binds us or holds us back. The Spirit of The Living God can bring us to life. Life is not in vain for us, no matter what we have been through or are struggling with now. Just receive the power of God to become an overcomer. I did, and it brought me through unthinkably difficult trials. God is able. Try Him and see for yourself. He never fails. He is God. He is for us. It doesn't matter who is against us. Greater is He who is in us than He who is in the world. Amen. And Praise God!

God is for us. He is with us, and in us. Even when we don't feel like it, God is still for, with and in us. We just have to trust Him, and follow His specific words of life in the bible and live by every word of God, not feelings, bad circumstances or negative thoughts. We have all the resources of God available to us to live the Christian life. We can't do it on our own, in the flesh, tempted by the devil to conform to the world. We need God to sustain us, Jesus to save us, and the Spirit of God to empower us to live on His level. It's not about us. It's about God in us. God in us is our hope of glory, now and forever.

Jesus is consistent. He will never leave us or forsake us. People let us down - but *not* Jesus. He lifts us up. He inspires us to be our best, and challenges us to seek first the kingdom of God. Human nature is very inconsistent. Sometimes we are up, sometimes we are down. Jesus, however, never gets weary. He is The Eternal Energy. He is one with The Father of All Creation. His grace is sufficient for our every need. His strength is made perfect in our weakness. Glory be to God!

The Lord Jesus connected time and eternity. He defined eternal life as knowing God, now and forever. We are not living in a disconnected world down here. This life is directly related to the next. Eternal life connects God and man, eternity and time, heaven and earth. It gives purpose to our labor on earth. Our purpose is to know God and enjoy Him forever. That makes even the meaningless struggles have purpose. Even suffering has meaning, since it prepares us for heaven. We learn patience, endurance and perseverance. Those qualities will get us ready to meet our Lord.

Authority. We all need authority. And many of those in authority on earth are not good, responsible leaders. Only Jesus was a good leader, because He did not use His authority, that is, all authority in Heaven and on earth, to be selfish. He only used His power to help hurting people. The

President of the United States or any country has limited authority, compared to Jesus. Jesus represents God. His will be done, in His timing. The Lord reigns, let the earth rejoice, let the people be glad. Though He allows man to rule for a season, He will step in at the right time, before man destroys himself, set up the Kingdom of God on earth, and Jesus will be Lord everywhere.

Accomplishment. Jesus accomplished more than any man ever, in just 33 years of life here on earth. He finished the work of salvation by dying on the cross to redeem us from sin and death. He reversed the curse hanging over us. He stripped Satan of his power of deceit. He brought us the eternal life connection to enjoy the rest of our lives here and in Heaven. His blood will never lose its power. It brings forgiveness and restoration to as many as receive Him. He, who began a good work in us, will be able to complete it, even when we blow it.

Qualified. Jesus is extremely qualified to be our Savior. He never sinned, though He was tempted at every point, just as we are. He resisted the temptation to live by bread alone. He chose to live by every word of God first, even during forty days of fasting. He refused to use His power for show, as in jumping off the temple. He would not bow to a fallen angel, the devil, even though the enemy offered Him the whole world. Man, that's standing on the promises in the pitfalls of life! We can do the same. As He is in the world, so are we, as we follow Him. Thank God!

17
TOUCHABLE, TESTED, THOROUGH AND TRUSTWORTHY

Jesus was touchable in that He was sympathetic to the point of crying for Lazarus. He got angry when the money changers were selling temple sacrifices for a profit. He was moved to caring when the little children were in His midst, and He beckoned them to come to Him. He was open to the Syrophoenician woman who crossed the border into Israel and pled with the Lord to heal her daughter. When He said she was out of bounds, as a Gentile, she pressed in to Him even more. Then she said that the outsiders eat whatever crumbs fall off the table. Jesus had compassion on her because of her faith, and her daughter was healed.

He was tested as He sweat drops of blood, agonizing in the Garden about dying for the sins of the world. Jesus prayed, "Not my will but Thine be done." His testing included dealing with twelve chosen men to be His Disciples who were impulsive, doubting and selfish. But He believed in them, not in their weak and selfish flesh, but in their potential when they followed Him and received His power to become fishers of men. We, too, have unlimited possibilities with God because He believes in us, even when we deny Him or doubt Him. We have to stay after Him and pursue Him, and not give in to the weaknesses of our flesh.

He was thorough. He cleanses us from all sin, as we confess our sins to Him. He has the power to forgive and restore us to righteous living. He will not give up on us. Let us dare not give up on ourselves. All things are possible with God. We just have to keep on pressing on to the prize of the high calling of God in Christ Jesus. We can overcome anything that holds us back from being our best, for The God who began a good work in us is able to complete it. We can constantly improve. It is not just us, it is Christ in us.

Jesus was trustworthy. He stated very clearly, "I am The Truth." We can trust Him with our lives here and our eternal destiny. Anything that does not come through Him is a lie. Satan is the father of all lies. We need to learn to discern what is true and what is not. Satan appeals to our weak flesh, and tries to get us to conform to this passing-away world. Jesus is building the kingdom of God in us, with righteousness, joy and peace by His strong Spirit.

18

JESUS IS SACRED

He said, "I and the Father are one." He is also eternal. He said, "Before Abraham was, I am." He has the power and authority to forgive sins. He will forgive our sins, when we confess to God through Him. His blood is adequate to cleanse us from all unrighteousness. He is thorough. He will 'thoroughly purge His threshing floor,' and we will come out of it purer than gold.

He is strong enough. He is able to keep us from falling, and to present us faultless before His presence with exceeding joy. This is supernatural strength. It is exactly what we need to follow Him. He was perfect on earth, and believes we can work in that direction as we draw strength from Him. Our human nature is still weak, but His spirit is stronger. Let us draw on Him for the power to overcome.

Jesus is powerful. He just spoke the word of healing and the centurion's servant was healed. He did it because of one man's faith, a man who was not even a Jew. It's the power of the word of God. What we say is what we get. We can speak the word of God, which is truth, and see miracles happen. The most relevant miracle is Jesus changing us into disciples when we are very undisciplined. He can do it because He believes in us, even when we are weak. That changes us. The Lord God and His Son, our Savior, believe in us. Praise God! Get up in faith and follow Him. He is worthy of our life commitment.

God is willing. A lot of people are waiting for God to do something because they are not sure it is His will to do good for us. The scripture states that He will not withhold any good thing from those who love Him. Jesus talked to the man with the withered hand who said, "If you are willing, you can." Jesus said emphatically, "I am willing. Stretch out your hand." We need to stretch out to where God is already moving in life helping helpless people. All things are possible to God. Let us get in the flow of good things happening as we have and speak faith in God.

19

HE IS ENOUGH, EXCLUSIVE AND FULFILLING

Jesus is enough. His grace is sufficient for every need. His strength is made perfect in our weakness. That is enough! We can make it with Him operating through us by His Spirit.

He is also exclusive! Jesus said, "I am the way." There are not many roads to the same God. The God of Creation and The Father of our Lord Jesus Christ make it clear that we are lost without them. Jesus came to offer "the way," to God. Not a way. Different religions try to reach God through different acts of man, like facing Mecca, bathing in the Ganges River, or doing a pilgrimage to Jerusalem. God doesn't require us to do anything to save ourselves. He saves us through the gift and sacrifice of Jesus the Son of God. No person can be saved by good works, otherwise God would have said His Son is only a way. Jesus is the way. Repent or perish is His cry.

The Lord is fulfilling. He fills the deep, God-shaped vacuum inside of all of us. And He fills us to overflowing with love, peace and joy. Nothing on this earth can do that!

People try every day to fill their lives with material things, more money, fame and popularity. Those are all vain things. Only God can fill the emptiness within our souls. He has done it through Jesus Christ our Lord. He fulfills us. Completely. Thank God.

20

CHALLENGING -- CREATIVE -- MEANINGFUL

Jesus challenges all of us to deny ourselves, take up our crosses and follow Him. This will bring out the best in us. The best, in the sight of God our Father and designer.

The Lord is creative. He makes all things new. Our past is over to Him. He forgives all and gives us a brand new start, at His expense. What an offer. We are wise to heed His leading and let Him make new creations out of us.

Jesus is meaningful. He came that we might have life more abundant. That is His kind of life. It goes far beyond what we experience with our senses here on earth. It is life on God's level, in the Spirit. It also satisfies our souls and gives purpose to our every step.

21

SALVATION WORK OUT

Salvation is the free gift of God through Jesus the Lamb of God who takes away the sins of the world. We must receive it with great joy and gratitude, and work it out, with fear and trembling. No! We don't work for salvation. We work it out. There is a huge difference here. Jesus finished the work for us. It is too expensive for us to pay, because we could never save ourselves. We are imperfect. God requires a perfect sacrifice for our sins. I would die for my own children and grandchildren. It would, however, do no good since my blood is not pure. I sin, I have sinned, and if I sin again, I have to confess and repent and be cleansed from all sin.

Jesus never sinned. He didn't disobey God the Father, even once. He is perfectly qualified to be the perfect sacrifice for the sins of the whole world. He was willing to go to the cross for us. He had no cross. He came all the way from heaven to gets ours. The gift goes on, The Father gave the Son. The Son gives the Spirit. The Spirit gives us life, so we can give the gift of love. The gift goes on, and on, and on.

Let us take up the cup of salvation and pour it out to others. We aren't saved to sit at home and watch football and soap operas. We are saved to tell others. We are witnesses unto Jesus the Christ, the Son of the Living God. Let's get it into gear. I don't have to be primed to tell you about my grandchildren. Neither do you, so, why don't we freely tell others about Jesus and the gap He filled with His own blood? Maybe it is because we don't realize its significance.

The early Christians in the Book of Acts could not help but tell of what they had seen and heard. They had seen 3,000 people saved when Peter preached after the coming of The Holy Spirit at Pentecost. They saw miracles happen when the Apostles spoke healing in the Name of Jesus, which is above all names. There was a riot everywhere the Disciples of Jesus went, for they would not accept the status quo, or conform to the world's view of God, as "The unknown God."

Paul said, "God is not far from any one of us. In Him we live, and move and have our being." That is a far cry from being "unknown." The early Christians marched right into the pit of doubt and unbelief and attacks by the Pharisees, who were legalists, regarding the law. The Christians were no legalists. They were set free people who penetrated the pagan world, and the religious world, with 'the truth,' that sets men free.

To get where they were, and get out of the huddle, the church building, we need to wait on God, receive the power from on high. Jesus talked about sending such power, after He ascended back into heaven. We are called to go into the entire world and preach the Gospel. The whole body of believers is to do the work of the ministry. Not just the pastors, teachers, evangelists, apostles and prophets. We are all ambassadors for Christ. We can communicate His love to others, in action and words.

In order to do it, we have to work out our salvation with fear and trembling. We need to stay on the cutting edge with the Lord. To always set Him before us. We are to dwell (stay) in His presence, being conscious of Him all throughout the day. To continue in Jesus' words of spirit and life. To discipline ourselves to follow The One Who Paid the Price for us. To give God our best effort and lay hold of Him, for that which He lay hold of us.

The price is paid for us, with the purifying blood of Jesus. Let's give back to God the love and energy He deserves. He gave first, His all. How can we give less? We are not earning anything here, just responding to the amazing love of God poured out for us in His awesome Son. Actually, He is more awesome than anyone who ever laid foot on this planet. He is more awesome in love. 'For God *so* loved the world, that He gave His only begotten Son that whoever believes in Him shall not perish but have everlasting life.' Praise The Father and the Son.

The price we need to pay is the price to keep our minds renewed on the truth, and not fall into the lies of the enemy. We need to make our feelings line up with the word of God. We need to get under, actually see ourselves under, the shadow of The Most High God, not under the circumstances. We can do it, for we are more than conquerors through the love and grace of Jesus the Christ. We can do all things through the deep, inner strength He gives us by His Holy Spirit.

It's a work out. Just as we work out our bodies with

exercise, we need to exercise our spirits. When we work out with prayer and praise and meditating on the truth, and speak it in faith, we overcome lethargy, coldness, depression, loneliness and low-self esteem. We are speaking of elevating to Christ-esteem now. That is who God says we are in Christ Jesus our Lord. When I was low, my spirit rose up high in what I discovered to be HIGHdentity. I dug into the truth of God's word and clung to who God said I was.

Feelings have to go when they are low. We can feel good about God, for He is good, and all things work for good for we who love Him and follow His purpose for us. As we discover who God is, we start having good feelings about Him. For He is our Exceeding Joy. He is the Rewarder of we who diligently seek Him. My earthly Daddy diligently worshiped God, and was the most diligent working man who became very successful, coming from a losing farm situation. But he did not wallow in his past. He pressed on to higher rewards. He persevered at his work, his worship and his family commitment, and he won. We, his family, were blessed. In fact, we continue to be blessed.

When we seek God with all our hearts, we find Him. We find out that He is our Father in heaven who is not willing for any one of His children perish. We discover that God is for us. What difference does it make that others are against us, or the devil is out to get us. God matters most. He is most interested in our working out our salvation He so freely gave to us.

22

BE TRANSFORMED

Being transformed is a process of renewing our minds on the truth of God's word. To renew means to stay fresh, to keep focused on the higher values of the Lord, not on the lower compromises of this world. We are what we think. We must think like God thinks to make it in life. That means we must renew our minds on the truth, not on what we see around us in the world.

We can have the mind of Christ, but not without digging into 'the word' and going for it big time. It is a developing process of getting to know the Lord. Jesus said we can "Know God through Him." To know Him we have to study His blood of truth and begin the process of understanding God.

Many people say they don't understand the bible. That is because they don't study it. As John Wesley said, "Scripture interprets scripture." The more we study, the more we know. The more we know, the more it fits together, like a puzzle becoming more complete.

We are to bring every thought captive to obedience to

Christ. That takes a lot of filling our minds with the truth, so we won't just sit around and fight off negative thoughts, coming from Satan or low thinking people in this world. Every thought is a big order, but we can do it, one step at the time. Finally our thinking is dominated by the truth.

By bringing every thought captive, we allow Christ to be formed in us. It is a process of gradually overcoming worldly thinking that is very limited in scope, with the higher thinking of the Lord through His eternal words. God's ways are not our ways, but they can become our ways when we bring every thought captive to obedience to Christ, thereby allowing Him to become formed in us. Then we become like the Lord, more and more, as we apply His truth to our everyday lives, thoughts, actions and responses.

The Christian life is not something we can do on our own. Many people would like to follow Jesus, but think it is too difficult, for He is a perfect man. Following Him is impossible for human beings without His radical help. That is the good news. We don't have to live the Christian life on our own. The Lord lives it through us. Although it is beyond our human comprehension, we still can do it. We do it by faith in God and the power of the Spirit of Christ living in us.

Actually, that is what the Bible is about. It's about the failure of men and women to live up to God's laws. That is exactly why He sent Jesus, to show us that it could be done. But first He had to atone for our failure to keep the law. The impossibility of God's law is that if we 'break it at only one point, we are guilty of breaking all.' God goes with perfection, or nothing else qualifies.

So, Jesus was the only One qualified to break the stronghold of the curse of sin and death, which was caused by our sin. He sacrificed His perfect life for our very imperfect ones. He became sin for us, though He never sinned, that we might become the righteousness of God through Him. We are righteous through His pure blood, which gives us a brand new start in living for Him, with all of our past sins forgiven.

Now that we are reconciled to God, by His own gift of salvation, we can start to live The Christian Life, not only with a new start, but also a new heart. That's a vital part of the new covenant that God makes with us. He says He will put a new heart "Within us." And we will be able to choose to obey and follow Jesus, not the dictates of our weak human flesh which is prone to sin and wander away from God.

Christ is being formed in us. We don't just change overnight. But we do change directions, and available power. Now we can start to win the victory over sin, both self and worldly allurements, plus the temptations of the devil. Now we can become like Christ Jesus our Lord. It is a process for the rest of our lives. The closer we get to Him, the more we walk in right choices.

Christians are not sinless. We just sin less. Our selfish natures begin to wind down to zero, as the life of our Risen Savior forms character in us. We become more loving, and less lustful for what our eyes see and our flesh desires. The pride we are born with begins to be broken.

We become humbled before God, realizing how far we fall short of His perfect will for us. But we don't wallow in self-pity, rather we take up the cup of salvation and drink deeply of His Spirit and ask Him to fill us with Himself and produce good fruit in us. Jesus humbled Himself. We usually have to be humbled by God, or by our own sins, and failure to keep our eyes on Him and His higher purpose for our lives.

Sin is already formed in us. The best way to get it out is to let Jesus be formed in us. We granted each of us a free will. We need to exercise it to follow the King of Kings and The Lord of Lords. We can choose to love or to lust, to forgive or to not forgive, and to have His joy or to let the little foxes spoil our day. To stay in strife with people or to be gentle and live in peace.

We get the scripture in our minds. We memorize the idea. We determine to 'let Christ be formed in us.' It's very simple. Challenging it is, but it is totally applicable to our lives. We are not too bad for God to change us. He will be formed in us if we believe Him and trust Him to change us. We just have to be determined to keep the faith, and keep the word of God built up on the sharper than any 2-edged sword.

23

CAN DO PEOPLE

Philippians 4:13 says "we can do all things through Christ who strengthens us." The potential we have in walking with the Lord is far beyond our own strength. It is Christ in us. He who began a good work in us will be able to complete it. The sky is not the limit with God. All things are possible with Him.

God is "All in All." He is not limited in any way. We have to get that into our thinking or we limit ourselves by focusing on our own weaknesses and failures, and those of the ones around us every day. Jesus overcame the world, the flesh and the devil; so can we. We have the same power available to us that raised Him from the dead. He can make new creations out of us. He can give us the direction and the power to follow Him in righteous living, and prepare to spend eternity with Him in heaven.

We can praise God. No matter what happens, we can praise Him. God inhabits the praise of His people. When we praise Him, He moves into our lives. Praise also works with human beings. We praise each other, and we get closer. We criticize each other, and we separate, driving each other away.

Job praised God and lived. His wife tempted him to curse God and die. Job made the right choice and God restored his seven children, his riches, his flocks and his herds after he was tried to the hilt. God deserves praise. He thrives on it. When we praise Him, He gravitates to us. We draw Him in.

We can keep our eyes on Jesus. It's hard in a world with many distractions, but we can do it. For we can do all things through Christ, our strength. When we do, we will see the way clearly, for He is the way. We will know the truth, and the truth will set us free, to be our best selves.

24

BROKEN

The Christian life is a wonderful experience. It is following the Christ, who is the Wonderful Counselor, the Mighty God, the Everlasting Father. Plus, He is The Prince of Peace. He is able to keep us from falling and to present us faultless before His presence with exceeding joy. Remember that the Lord is our exceeding joy. We can make it through life standing up against all the obstacles and trials we face by keeping our eyes on Him, who is the Author and Finisher of our Faith.

Nevertheless, we have to be broken before God to walk with Him. Otherwise, we think we are able to keep ourselves from falling into temptation and sin. Temptation is not a sin in itself, for Jesus Himself was tempted by the enemy. He resisted, but our flesh is weak, even as Christians. It is actually easier to give in to the desires of our human nature than to resist and stand against them.

We must deny ourselves, take up our cross and follow Jesus. Yet, we are only denying ourselves worldly pleasures that pass away, and enslave us, and never really satisfy the deep longing in our souls for ultimate fulfillment. God fills us full to overflowing. His very presence is enough to satisfy our longing hearts. I know I experienced that fulfillment as a child, a teenager and as a young adult growing up in a Christian home. I was raised by Christian parents and surrounded by family with a strong Christian influence all around me.

God only tells us to deny ourselves the lusts of the eyes and flesh to find something far better: The fruit of His Spirit operating in us. That includes love, joy and peace. We cannot have both. It is a problem, because we try to straddle the fence, and take God in one hand and the world in the other. Jesus emphatically said, and lived like it cannot be done. We either give ourselves to worldly things or to God. The one we give ourselves to controls us. God brings us righteousness and peace and joy. The world only gives us a dying vine, when its pleasures are all over with.

Jesus set a perfect example for us. He humbled Himself. He denied Himself all the worldly pleasures, and his own flesh. He refused to be selfish. We don't seem to have any problem with being self-centered. Just look at children. It's all about them. Unless someone, namely their parents, teach them to be unselfish, and that they are not the only ones in this world, they will wind up self-obsessing, and becoming totally frustrated, and empty. 'Things' alone just cannot satisfy the human soul. Only God Himself can, on the spiritual level.

After we deny ourselves the constant gratification the world offers, we must take up our cross. That means crucify our selfish desires, just as Jesus did. Be crucified with Him, as in getting 'self' out of the picture so we can follow Him. That is, put others first. Meet people's needs. Do good things for them. Be kind to them. Reach out to hurting people all around us. Spend time with people who are alone. Take them food. But most of all, share the love of Jesus with them. Lead them to the light of God's word. Speak the encouraging words of the bible to them. There is no such thing as too much encouragement for anyone.

Being broken before God also means we have a teachable spirit. God can direct us when we listen to Him and read His word for guidance. That can be tough in a self-directed society. But not impossible. For all things are possible with God. We must 'trust in the Lord with all our hearts, and lean not unto our own understanding. In all our ways acknowledge Him, and He will direct our paths.' Be still and know that He is God, and He has a plan for all of us. His purpose is very rewarding.

25

BLESSED WITH EVERY SPIRITUAL BLESSING

We are blessed by God with every spiritual blessing in Christ Jesus. That meets every need we could possibly have, and even needs we may not be aware of in this world of limited perspective. Secular people have a worldly vision that only deals with the temporary things of this life. God has an eternal kingdom vision that deals with our eternal spirits.

It all starts with forgiveness. Before we can be free to enjoy life, we have to get rid of the burden of sin and guilt and condemnation. Jesus did that for us on the cross. He forgives all our sins, according to Psalm 103. Sometimes we feel like we aren't worthy to be forgiven, and we certainly treat people who hurt us badly that way. The good news is that we don't have to be worthy or deserve what God gives us. He is extremely merciful and forgiving is His very nature. He forgives us before we sin. He already knows us from our mother's womb. He has already provided for our forgiveness, which frees us up to live without guilt and condemnation. He frees us to forgive others, as God forgives us, not as we wrongly think they deserve.

Next is healing. God heals all our diseases. It is very inclusive, but we serve an inclusive God. He includes us in healing, which is totally His thing. Jesus healed all who were 'oppressed by the devil.' The enemy wants us to think God won't heal just because we aren't healed instantaneously, or we aren't healed at all. That's wrong. Sometimes God heals instantly -- that is a miracle. Miracles do happen. Oftentimes, He heals over a period of time, like in a wound healing. Healing is God's call. By Jesus' stripes we are healed. We just need to wait on God's timing and learn to trust Him. He is in charge of eternity. We can trust the Lord who sacrificed Jesus for our eternal salvation.

Then comes redemption from destruction. That's a big one, too. The bible says we are "Destroyed by a lack of wisdom." When we get cut off from the Lord, we lose, big time. It can lead to bitterness and despair. With God the Father and Jesus the Son, we are redeemed from destruction. Nothing can destroy us as we stay close to Him. Jesus said, "Abide in me." That means we are to 'Set the Lord always before us; because He is at our right hand, we will not be moved.' As we dwell in the secret place of meditation of His word, we are protected by Almighty God.

We are also, crowned with loving kindness and tender mercies. His loving kindness is better than life. One day in His presence is better than a thousand anywhere else. Praise God! He is forever kind, loving, forgiving and merciful. We will lack no good thing when we walk with Him. For in His presence is fullness of joy. At His right hand are pleasures forevermore. Glory to God in the highest, for bringing us loving kindness in the lowest places.

Best of all, God satisfies us with good things, so that our strength is renewed like the eagle's. Now that is power we need to live life more abundant. God is for us. We need to remember this, no matter how hard it gets in life's maze of trials. We are being tested, Psalm 11. God has every right to test us, and see if we really want Him, or just what He gives us. Selfishness has to go to follow Jesus. We can give and give to others and live above the emptiness of the material world. God satisfies us to help satisfy others. Amen.

We are extremely blessed to have access to God. That means we get grace instead of judgment. We get love instead of punishment. We are taught to "Come boldly," into the very presence of God. And what a blessing that is. God is personal. He is not an impersonal force of nature. He is not Mother Nature. He is Father God. And He invites His children by creation to come into His personal presence by salvation, through the love of Jesus Christ our Lord. We are invited to be a part of God's 'forever family fellowship.' Thank Him!

26

DELIVERED TO STAND

Jesus came to deliver us from evil. He gives us authority over Satan and all the powers of darkness. Jesus is far above all principality and power, and wickedness in high places. There are really demons of fear, lust, depression, anger and unforgiveness. Yet, we have the advantage over Satan by being forgiven by God. This is how we can forgive others, immediately. Satan is prevented from taking advantage over us with unforgiveness.

God wants us in good relationship with Himself, ourselves and others. A big part of evil is that it can keep us from healthy connections with God, others, even with ourselves. We must never allow evil get a stronghold on us, by choosing to stay angry with God or others, even with ourselves. Whenever we get locked down by a stronghold of fear or anger or depression, we can break it by "Pulling down strongholds." We have that authority in Jesus' Name.

We must stand against the wiles of the devil. That

means after we put on the whole armor of God. We must never fight the enemy naked. We must take up the shield of faith, and quench the fiery darts of the enemy. Then we can keep anger and unforgiveness and lust and depression and grudges, etc., out of our lives. We are equipped by God to win in the battle with evil. The best way to stand against the enemy of our souls is to put on the full armor of God. Otherwise, we are fighting the king of deception, lies and fear in the spiritual nude. No, no! God has already fully equipped us to stand on The Rock, Jesus Christ. He gives us the weapons to do it. It's like getting dressed spiritually.

First, we must put on the belt of truth. The truth of God stands forever. His word is forever settled in heaven. Plus, Jesus is the personal embodiment of the truth. We are really standing on who He is. He is the same, yesterday, today and forever. He ever lives to coach us from heaven. His holy presence through His Spirit guides us into all truth. Our minds are opened by Him to who we are in Christ, which gives us HIGHdentity, which is more important than anything we have on this earth.

The greatest part of the truth is that Jesus extends it to us and tells us to live by every word of God, as He did. His word shields us so we don't fall for any deception or lies of the enemy. We are to only speak The Truth. His very words are spirit and life. We can speak life into very lifeless situations. For the word of God is 100% effective. It never fails to produce encouragement and life when people are in bondage to anything evil.

The truth of God is sharper and more effective than any two-edged sword. It will penetrate any darkness with the light of God, in the name of Jesus. The Light of God penetrates any stronghold of the evil powers of darkness

with light, which is hope. The word of God brings
deliverance from evil. We have the authority to speak life in
Jesus' name. When people are depressed, we speak
encouragement and the 'more than Conqueror' possibility,
in the name of the Lord.

I was facing clinical depression at one time in my life.
I was never really depressed, but I was fighting a very tough
battle with negative thoughts for my own personal identity.
That's when I discovered HIGHdentity. I believed God
when His word says we are "More than conquerors." My
feelings were very low, my emotions shot with rejection and
failure, my job situation was uncertain, I was losing money
trying to get a Christian book store going, but I stood on
God's word about who we are in Christ: More than
conquerors. I fed that truth into my emotions and soul until
I got it deep inside, and overcame all the garbage about
feelings of failure, and rejection.

I refused to let my circumstances, my low feelings
and a fallen angel tell me I was a failure. I believed I was an
overcomer through the Love of Jesus, and I stood on it
through hell's attack and high water. Then, I started
walking on the water with Jesus, in the spiritual sense, of
course. The more I fed my spirit the truth the stronger I got
in the Lord. When we are walking with The Master of Our
Souls, His strength is made perfect in our weakness. We feel
weak in our flesh, but we are strong in the Lord.

It is not too late to fill your attacked mind with the
truth. Jesus said, "The truth will set you free" but we have to
continue in His word. Press on. Reject all the draining
thoughts the enemy floods us with. 'When the enemy comes
in like a flood, the Lord will raise up a standard against
him." This standard is His eternal, 100% effective, 2-edged

sharp, soul-piercing, Satan-stripping word of God sword. It worked for Jesus. It will work for anyone of us who renews his or her mind on it, gets fortified enough to speak it and pull down the strongholds of evil that bind us.

Jesus said, "The truth will set you free!" We are bought with the blood of Jesus to be free. Free from negative thoughts, for God's thoughts and words to us are always positive and full of promise, no matter how low we get or feel. We are free, in Christ, to be what God intended us to be. Full of life and zest and enthusiasm and joy and peace and love. Anything less than that needs to be debunked.

Another vital part of the armor of God is the breastplate of righteousness. We need to put it on in our minds and spirits so we can resist the mocking of the enemy that we are failures. We are righteous in the sight of Almighty God through the pure blood of Jesus, The Lamb of God who takes away the sin of the world. See yourself as righteous. I did. Even when I felt down and like a failure. There is no way to fail standing in the blood covenant with God through His sin offering for our sins through Jesus. The covenant is here to stay. Stay with it. Remind your emotions that you are righteous by the grace of God.

Put on the helmet of salvation. Protect yourself against low feelings of not being saved. We are not saved by feelings. We are saved by grace, the sacrifice of Jesus for us. That is forever settled in heaven. It is a covenant sealed in blood for all to see and know and stand in. The Holy Spirit bears witness with our spirits that we "Are the children of God." Plus, the word of god is written that we may "Know we are saved." Our emotions will line up with this assurance when we make our emotions line up with the truth.

The sword of The Spirit, the word of God -- take it up. Cut through the lies of the devil. When he reminds you of your past, remind him of his future. When he says you can't make it, say "I can do all things through Christ who gives me inner strength." When the enemy says, "Has God said?" Say "Yes! God has said that I am 'More than a Conqueror,' not a failure. Get behind me Satan, in the Name of Jesus!"

Be shielded from the evil darts the enemy throws at us. Pick up the shield of faith. Just hold up the shield which is the truth of God. It will quench the fiery darts of Satan, for Satan makes war against the saints, those of us who are following Jesus the Christ.

To really be at peace, put on the shoes of peace. God has made peace with us through the blood of the cross, His own Son sacrificed for our sins. Be at peace, with God, others and your most inner self, thus His peace will surpass all understanding. It will keep us from getting offended. "Great peace have we who love Thy Word, O God, and nothing shall offend us." Psalm 119:65.

27

ETERNAL PURPOSE

Most people try to find their purpose in a job, vocation, position in life, making more money, getting promoted by mere man, living in a dream house, and being entertained. The problem is that we can never get enough of those things to fill the hole in our souls. We are made for God, and nothing but God can satisfy the inner groaning and longing of our souls.

We are created by God to live life more abundant, because of what Jesus did for us on the cross. To serve others and be ambassadors for Christ to let people know Jesus broke the curse hanging over us and gives us the eternal blessing. Then we can live to glorify God in all we do. Now that is purpose galore. It's not about self-indulgence. Self-indulgence is the devil's lie and of the world. It's about receiving from God and giving to others the greatest news ever heard by human ears. Thank God, we have something that is so good it is more important than what we say about our grandchildren even. It is good news.

Three men were working on building a church.

Someone asked each of them what they were doing. The first said he was "Laying brick." The second said he was, "Making $15 an hour." The third said he was, "Building a Cathedral." The first two were rather short sighted and had little purpose past the challenge of laboring and the temporary lift of money. The third had eternal purpose in that He was doing something far bigger than his own labor or his reward in money. He was working to build a house of worship to the Eternal God of this universe, who is the Father of All Mankind. What vision. We are the Temple of God who lives in us.

Our purpose can be as adventuresome as God is. He is our Father and will not withhold any good thing from those who love and follow Him. He is The Creator of All Things, and all people. His purpose is for us to become one in Christ Jesus. Otherwise, we are fighting for self and self always divides us. Jesus unites us with a bond that is closer than breathing, and nearer than hands and feet. It is far beyond just getting together to eat. It is being united in celebrating the eternal fact that we are bought with a High price: the blood of The Son of God. He adopts us into His family. We celebrate! That is what life and worship is all about.

Purpose is also buttressed by an attitude of gratitude. It is so great to have a God who is great, and greatly to be praised. An atheist's worst moment is when he feels grateful, and has no one to thank. That is awfulness enthroned. Conversely, gratitude to God is purpose enthroned. He is enthroned in the praises of His people. We are saints to God, His own special people, called out of darkness to declare the praises of Him who has shown His eternal light on us in Jesus, The Light of The World.

Purpose grows much higher when we realize we are called to declare the praises of God. He inhabits the praise of His People. Praise draws God close to us. Praise also draws any human close to us. Criticism drives them away. Criticism, complaining and blaming God drives Him far away. He responds and comes near to praise. He deserves it. Having a God big enough and good enough to praise at all times is purpose. Praise The Lord!

Purpose includes praising God for who He is. He is good. All things work for good for those who love Him. No matter how bad it looks or gets down here. God is still good. He brings good out of bad. He allows us to be 'chastised,' to purify us. He allowed Job, a righteous man, to be tested. God tests the righteous. But Satan tempts us to, 'curse God and die.' The Lord God wants us to, 'praise Him and live.'

Purpose is having eternal life, which is 'knowing God.' We can know Him personally through Jesus the very personal Son, who was born of a virgin, took on weak human nature, and overcame the world and the devil. We can be like Him, for 'creator is He who is in us, than He who is in the world.' God actually shares His greatness, His love, His mercy, His loving kindness, His very being with us. We can find meaning in everything in knowing God lifts us over the obstacles and gives us something far beyond the limitations of this world.

We can find temporary meaning in work, fun, friends, and entertainment in this world. It all ends in frustration because it doesn't last. God's purpose for us lasts forever. He is forever our Father who blesses us with life more abundant in Christ. We have heaven to look forward to. This life is wonderful following The Wonderful Counselor,

Mighty God, Everlasting Father and Prince of Peace. It prepares us to live with Him in heaven forever. No eye could imagine how good it will be. No mind could conceive how good God will be to live with. No ear has heard the celestial sounds we will hear in Heaven. No heart could take in the glory of it all down here. It will be worth it all, when we see Jesus. This is eternal purpose. Praise the name of Jesus.

28

ADJUST TO GOD'S VIEWPOINT

God the Almighty is in control of this world and the entire universe. His Will is going to be done. His permissive will is in effect for now. He is Longsuffering, not willing anyone perish. His long-range goal is that we all come to maturity, which is coming to a thorough knowledge of Jesus Christ so that we are perfectly at peace with each other. There is still a lot of strife in life that has to be changed into peace. This is possible only by the Prince of Peace Himself.

Jesus is the way to God the Father. God will not permit any other way. All religions are false that do not exalt Jesus as Savior and Lord. Jesus is the only name given under heaven whereby we may be saved. People must adjust to God's way or perish! Jesus said it plainly, "If all of you don't repent, you will perish." Nobody could say that strong statement unless He had the authority of God. Jesus did. He was one with The Father.

Suffering purifies. We try to avoid it, but we must learn to take it as a part of our preparation to live with God one day. God will bring us through it. Jesus suffered as no man ever did. He made it through Calvary, and He can pull us through anything we face, if we follow Him, by keeping our eyes on Him and obeying Him.

Obedience is better than sacrifice. When we don't obey God's wisdom, we pay the price. We hurt ourselves and drag others into the pit of suffering with us. We can get better. We must obey God, even if it means opposing men's lack of wisdom.

The peaceable fruit of righteousness is what God is developing in us. He chastises us so He can get rid of every spot and wrinkle, for Jesus is coming back for a prepared bride, His body, the church. No unrighteousness is allowed in heaven. Fornication and adultery must be repented. Homosexuality is an abomination to God. It is totally backwards of His plan for one man and one woman to be in wedlock together. No aberrations allowed.

Liars are not accepted. Jesus is the truth. He expects all of us to get rid of all lies and tell only the truth. For the truth sets people free. Lies deceive us and mislead us. Jesus is the way. He would never mislead anyone. We are talking about the huge issue of finding God's way to eternal life and heaven. Jesus is the only way. He is not a religion. He is the revelation of God to mankind. God was in Christ, reconciling the world unto Himself -- without compromise.

Cowards are not in with God. Jesus was the bravest man who ever lived. He sacrificed His earthly life, after He gave up His heavenly privilege to come here. He sacrificed Himself for us, so we could be eternally united with our Father in heaven. Being a coward is a no with Him. He challenges us to be brave like Him. "Fear not," He stated emphatically, over and over. Being of good courage is our choice, following a brave and courageous Savior.

God expects us to be faithful in little things, while He will advance us to greater things. Responsibility starts where we are, not where we want to be. We can begin to be faithful right where we are, even when we have been irresponsible. If we want a better job, be faithful to our present job. When we want a better marriage, we need to be faithful to 'do unto our mate what we wish they would do unto us.' Making demands is out; doing our best is in. God will reward us, because He is a rewarder of those who diligently seek Him.

Perseverance is what God is about. We are in life for the long run. Eternity is too long to be wrong. Jesus is right, "He who endures to the end will be saved." To endure we must build up our spiritual stamina by staying close to God through meditation day and night. We must develop the mind of Christ in us. We have to keep reading His words until we get them in our spirits and build endurance.

Jesus put us on the starting line by offering us the gift of eternal salvation. We must work it out with awesome reverence for God and appreciation to Jesus for giving His all for us. He, who began a good work in us, will not be able to complete it until we arrive in The Father's house. We need to fight the good fight, keep the faith and finish the course. It's so simple when we follow our Father's wise directions through His Son. We can make it to the finish, but we must continue in the word of God. We must resist following our flesh and the allurements of this world.

29

BEGIN NEW NOW

The Christian life is not going on as we are in our natural state of sin. It is taking on the supernatural. We can't follow a Spiritual God when we are following the dictates of our weak human flesh, surrounded by the temptations to indulge and over-indulge in the things of this world. We have to start new with repentance. Repent or repentance is a good word, for it means to leave the dimension of limitation, and enter the kingdom of God, which has no limitation.

We are new -- in Christ. We don't just turn over a new leaf. We enter a new life with God. In His own superior wisdom and power and mercy, He pours Himself into us through His Holy Spirit. We can be just as new and full of Him as we choose to be. He does not allow Luke warmness. He has given too much to us in Christ Jesus. He has sacrificed for us. He expects us to give our total human effort to follow Him and His way. When we make that turn to Him, to listen and follow His wisdom, He energizes us. He will not energize us living in sin.

Following Jesus is receiving and giving. God gives, we receive, but He expects us to give, too. 'Give and it will be given,' is His Law. We are not receivers of eternal life, at the expense of Jesus, to just sit down on our salvation. We are to go into all the world and help make the world new. That new can begin to happen when we present the possibility to others that they can become new, too. We share newness, not the past pain all the time. We need to put the emphasis on what people can become, including ourselves, not just what we have been through.

God's only qualification for us to be new is that we be 'diligent' to follow Him. We need to lay hold of Jesus for that which He lay hold of us. He bought us with His blood, to make us new. To give us a fresh start with God and life. We must 'seek first His kingdom, and all else will be added.' In other words, we are to cultivate our inner souls in relationship with God. Get spiritual is what we need to do. The world tries to squeeze us into its mold of 'getting physical.' We don't need any help in doing that. Our flesh is weak. The world is too much with us. Plus, our enemy is out to get us with the deceitfulness of the riches of this world.

We have to become new in Christ. In our natural state, we don't understand the things of God; when we are born of God's Spirit, we begin to understand the Lord and His ways. His ways are not our ways, but we can learn His ways by hungering and thirsting for righteousness. The Spirit of God gives us the new start now when we receive Him into our lives. We must keep the fire burning by staying on the Emmaus Road with Jesus, listening to His words, which are spirit and Life.

The greatest problem we face may be spiritual

starvation. We allow our souls to dry up because we don't feed them the word of God to keep us built up. We must stay fresh and new. We can since we can do all things through Christ our Lord.

The old way of life has to go when we line up with The Lord. We have to give up our lusts and pride and selfishness. Self and service don't fit. We are called to serve. Jesus did all the time. He lived to heal, save and deliver people from evil, and the terrible consequences which follow. He said, "Follow me, and I will make you fishers of men." When we become new in Him, and stay new by disciplining ourselves to work through whatever hinders or blocks us off from our best selves, we set the example for others to become new.

We can begin to be an example of newness now. Our past is forgiven; it is under the blood of Jesus. How dare anyone bring it up? We dare not bring up our own past or anyone else's, lest we extend the burden of some former failure. Our witness is about Jesus, not ourselves. We need God in our lives every day just as much as the ones who have fallen away and quit trying. So, we need to point people to Jesus Christ, who is the same, yesterday, today and forever. He is able to keep us from falling into the same pit over and over. He is God, and He is for us.

30

BRING EVERY THOUGHT CAPTIVE

For us to bring every though captive is a big order. It sounds impossible at first but God really means it when He teaches us that in 2 Corinthians 10. It starts right where we are, one thought at a time. It feels overwhelming, but we don't live by feelings. We live by facts, eternal facts, which overcome low feelings. Feelings aren't facts anyway. They come and go with the moment. The eternal facts of God's word are here to stay -- they work. They are totally functional.

We have to start where we are, right in the middle of a negative thought war. That's where I was when I was going through the roughest times of my life. The thought occurred to me that I could lose my mind to negative thinking, but I realized that I must begin to take control of my thinking, and follow the goal of bringing every thought captive.

I began the excruciating battle of getting my mind soaked with the truth, the facts. I quit just trying to fight the negative thoughts the enemy was throwing at me like machine gun fire. I listened to the word of God being said or sung on my tape player. I was tired from working hard all day. But as I lay on the floor, I soaked up the truth of God, and found out who I really am: a person in charge of my own thinking, and responsible for what I allow to stay in my mind.

We can't keep a negative thought from entering our mind, but we sure can keep it from staying there. For example, when the thought of, "I am so depressed" came into my mind, I would never agree with it. I would say out loud, as weak as I felt, "I am not depressed. I am impressed with Jesus Christ." This gave me the power to think up and not down.

It can be done. Just start with your own mind and don't allow any negative thoughts to stay there. You can do it, one thought at the time. God will help you and guide you. Just keep filling your mind up with the truth of God and it will overcome the negative. Good overcomes evil -- that is a fact. Praise God!

31

DE-GRIPPING THE GRASSHOPPER MENTALITY

When the Israeli spies went into the promised land to check it out, they came back with the report that the land was full of giants. That was not the problem. The problem was, they saw themselves as grasshoppers. That is the people of God, in covenant with The Almighty, getting such a low image of themselves. How vividly the tradition has passed down through the ages.

Today it is the labels put on people, like "convict," "divorcee," "repeat offender," "no good." "never amount to anything," or "disgrace to this family." God never puts those labels on us. Only judgmental people who don't understand God's faith in what He can do with hurting people, judge them and say they are incorrigible. After I went through divorce, a pastor told me that he would not want me to speak to his people because I was "divorced." I told him, I was divorced many years before, and I was not wearing that label, but I was wearing the label of "more than conqueror."

We have to stand up to people who are ignorant of what God can do in anyone's life to change them into the image of Christ, and let Christ be formed in them. There are no failures to God. Nobody is beyond His reach. Not a soul on this earth is too far gone. Jesus can change anyone willing and believing into being an 'overcomer.' He said in His revelation to the seven churches, "Blessed are the overcomers. They will be given a crown of life."

Now we have to get rid of the grasshopper mentality that has infected the human race with doubt and judgment on human mistakes and sins and believe people can change......with God's mighty help. Jesus came for that very reason, not just for the so called, 'good people.' Good people are not perfect themselves who are more morally straight on the outside, than people who do bad outward things like raping. Killing, stealing, assaulting and hurting other people. They have to repent of falling short of the glory of God, as in sinning, not being perfect, just like the offenders who release their anger on others.

Everyone needs Jesus equally in the sense that we are all under the curse of sin and death and imperfection. That's why everyone has to come to God, not through self-righteous good works, like the Pharisees, but through the cross of Jesus, and receive His righteousness as a gift. It is impossible for anyone to be saved on his or her own merits, since we all are less than 100% perfect. Jesus was 100% perfect. Everyone who breathes needs His righteous gift of salvation, whether we are 20% moral or 90% moral. All have sinned. All need the grace of God to save them from the wrath of God against sin.

I learned to see myself as an overcomer through Christ Jesus, especially when I was rejected, left my ministry in the church, opened a Christian book store and went into great debt for the first time. All of that overwhelmed me. It did not overwhelm God or His grace for me. I believed His word, that I could live like an overcomer, whether my circumstances were worthy or not, whether my feelings were at rock bottom or not.

The good news is that God meets us at the bottom, that's why Jesus came down -- down from His Glory in heaven -- to lift us up out of the pit of despair at not being good enough to save ourselves. Jesus told about the prodigal son who got his inheritance early, went into the far country, and wasted it all on reckless living. He did not repent and come home until he was so deficit that he was literally eating with the pigs.

Then he got up out of the slop, and took the first step to return to his father. He remembered that his father was merciful and wanted him back, and met him halfway as he desperately came back home. We need to remember that our father, the Father of our Lord Jesus Christ, is merciful, as well. He is in the redemption business. He wants to save us from ourselves, our selfish nature which will self-destruct on lust, pride, anger, unforgiveness and revenge, etc.

All of us have a deficit problem. Jesus reverses the deficit and wants to bring us back into the Father's family and put a robe on our backs, we are royalty to God, even though we sin. He will put a ring on our finger meaning we are in a blood Covenant with Him through Jesus. He will supply all our needs for eternity and we can eat at His bountiful table, free of charge, because He is a God of grace. His grace is sufficient for every need we have. The whole world has. Our God will provide.

32

GET OUT OF THE HOLE

People get stuck in the hole of debt, anger, frustration, loneliness, depression, hiding from responsibility, blaming the past which was imperfect. Everyone's past is imperfect. Nobody had perfect parents. I had strong Christian parents and still went through divorce, rejection, debt and fought depressing thoughts constantly. I almost got buried.

Turning to the God of my mother and father saved me. I was raised in a very Christian home. It was not perfect, but always working on it. I knew where to turn. I was a preacher for 25 years and knew the word of God. I just didn't know how to use it to overcome the heavy duty problems I was under.

Finally, I got under the shadow of God. Finally, I began to see myself as under the Lord's umbrella of protection from the evil thoughts that could destroy me and make me be depressed. No sir, I was never depressed. Everybody faces depressing thoughts at times, but I was facing what counselors call, "The big two: rejection and failure." I got out of the hole with the devil and his condemning thoughts because I believed I was who God said I was. The enemy can attack anyone, but he makes war against the saints, those of us who are trying to walk with God and be responsible.

See yourself as under the shadow of God. Get into HIGHdentity vision. Believe it; stand on it. Don't give in to thoughts of failure and rejection. God will never reject us or consider us failures. He thinks we are all worth redeeming from the claws of sin and destruction. He paid the price to set us free.

To get under the shadow of God, we must 'dwell' in His word and presence. We must soak up His truth until we are so saturated with Him and His love that we feel good about Him, and who we are in Him. It takes time and determination while working against all odds. It is worth the effort, for the end result is 'the peaceable fruit of righteousness for those who are trained by it.'

We all need to repent of entertaining destructive thoughts. That is the first step in getting out of the hole. Rise up in your mind, no matter where you are, or what you are facing. See yourself as God sees you. He sacrificed His son on the cross for all of us. Lay hold of Him. Press on to the prize of the high calling of God in Christ. Refuse to be held back. Don't let a fallen angel tell you who you are. Satan will destroy you. The better alternative is to believe God. Get up and go again, even when everything around you is falling apart. Even when you don't know what to do, just trust God.

Jesus has all authority in Heaven and on earth. He uses His power to help us, to lift us up out of the pitfalls of life. He can and He will. We just need to use our free will to agree with Him, not our low feelings or bad circumstances. Accomplishing this we can start where we are, no matter how low we are, and start rising up. We are talking about being helped by the one who made it through Calvary and suffered death on the cross, without giving up -- for us. Get the same mentality and put your faith in The Lord of Glory. He is for you!

33

SOMETHING TO LOOK FORWARD TO

I believe that all of us need something to look forward to, not just a job, vocation, home or travel destination. We need something big enough to put a spring in our steps, a joy in our souls and a song in our hearts.

We have it. In the coming of Jesus for His body, the church, us, who love and look forward to His appearing. Many people in the past have mistaken His coming as an escape from this life. How far off they were. We don't have to escape life; we have already passed from death into life by connecting with God through Jesus. This fact is clear from John 5:24. We can live joyful lives every day, not just because we have homes and money to do enjoyable things or have cars to ride in and people to love us down here.

We can be in a state of hedista, which is the Greek word for exceedingly glad. It was the word I found in the Greek dictionary in the 70's, looking for the name of our youth singing group in Albany. I still like it. Because God is our "Exceeding Joy," Psalm 43. He is able to do "Exceedingly abundantly above all we ask or think." He is willing, for He will not withhold any good thing from those of us who love Him and follow His purpose for our lives.

Jesus emphatically said that He would come again, and receive us unto Himself. We will forever be with the Lord. Now that is a once in a lifetime special event to look forward to; not to escape down here. We already have a foretaste of glory," by experiencing the love and presence of God moving in our hearts daily. But we have to dwell in His secret place, to realize the impact of His being closer than breathing, and nearer than hands and feet.

When Jesus comes back to earth He will receive us to himself. We will be caught up to meet Him and all the saints in the air. He will destroy the anti-Christ, who has the whole world under his sway, with the breath of His mouth. The words of our Savior are still more powerful than a mighty wind. He will just say 'the word!' He has all authority and power in Heaven and on earth. He delegates it to us so we can speak life in Jesus' Name.

It will be worth it all, when we see Jesus. He is the one special person we can look forward to meeting and living with forever. It is not based on our imagination; it is based on the forever settled-in-heaven word of God. All sorrow will be turned into joy. It can start here when we keep our eyes on Jesus in our spirits. There will be no more pain. What relief! No more death. We are born again to live eternally, for we are born of God's spirit, and He is eternal.

I am so glad we have someone to praise. Jesus the Christ, the Son of the Living God. Psalm 2 says to, "Kiss the Son." We can do that in spirit right where we are by praising Him and lifting up His name, the only name given under heaven by which we can be saved. We can glorify Him by telling people who are lost how great a savior He is. We can follow Him as Lord because He is worthy of our total commitment.

Eye has not seen, ear has not heard, neither has it entered into the heart of man, what God has prepared for those who love Him. Jesus said, "I go to prepare a place for you, that where I am, you may be also." I cannot think of any place I had rather be, than with Jesus Christ, the most deserving, courageous, sacrificial man who ever lived. He still lives to make intercession for us. He is ultimately concerned about the family of God. He gave all He had, Himself, His perfection, His love, and His body, to demonstrate God's love for a lost humanity.

In addition to going to be with The Lord in heaven, we can have heaven on earth. We have life more abundant in Him. We have authority over evil. We are loved with an everlasting love. We are saved from the wrath of God against sin by the pure blood of Jesus. The joy of The Lord is our deep, inner strength. We enter His gates with thanksgiving (thank God we have a Father in heaven to thank for every spiritual blessing and material blessing He pours out on us). We enter His courts with praise.

God is Great, and greatly to be praised! That is high worship. To get lost in wonder, love and praise." We can worship God in spirit and in truth. It's not determined by how many people are there. Where two or more are gathered, the Lord is present with us in spirit, for He is the one free spirit. It's better than going to a football game and cheering for our team who is winning with 100,000 people shouting at the top of their lungs. When the game ends the shouting dies down.

It is different with worshiping God. The Psalms say after we die, we will "Still be praising Him." Heaven will be like a giant, continuous praise rally. We have a cause that is worthy of eternal praise and worship, because the cause is the salvation of all mankind. Heaven rejoices when one soul is saved. We will rejoice that we made it to be with God and Jesus forever. We will know as we are known. Praise God. Let the celebration begin and never end!

34

DON'T LET ANYONE BLOW YOU OUT

The most helpful, applicable scripture in the area of dealing with people, especially irritating people who could offend you, is found in Psalm 119:165. The truth given there is, "Great peace have we who love thy word, O God, and nothing shall offend us." I have read that verse a few times in my life, but it suddenly came alive to me after I heard Dr. Gary Smalley ask the question on a video on relationships I was watching. I wasn't paying much attention until he said, "How would you like to be at the place where nobody could do anything to blow you out!" I jumped up! Yes! I would.

A short time later I ran across Psalm 119 where verse 165 grabbed my undivided attention. It said the same thing he was saying. It also parallels 1 Corinthians 13, The Love Chapter, which says, "Love is not easily provoked." Well, love may not be easily provoked, but human nature is 'easily provoked.' Every time I read that passage at a wedding I would cringe, for I knew that unless a couple knows this principle and applies it, they are in deep trouble, and will very often get their feelings hurt, and withdraw from each other, and pout, and harbor anger that will eat them alive unless they release it in a soft tone of voice way.

I learned a very important truth. I think it is the peak point in relationships, and self-control. As a friend of mine so well says, "We come unglued." That's exactly what happens when we don't know how to, above all, guard our hearts. We are over-reactors who take things personally and puff up with anger. Usually over nothing, depending on who is calling the shots. What one person thinks is nothing may cause another to consider it as major surgery.

I have found that I need to be on the alert all the time and not let anyone hurt my feelings. Learning to disagree agreeably is the key. We don't have to agree on the color or arrangement of a room, or whether or not we are going to a certain event or not. Heart surgery this is not. What we do need to agree on is our belief in God, the Father of our Lord Jesus Christ, the authority of His word, the bible, and grow in grace and understanding of how to live the Christian life in peace and the bond of love.

People who don't know how to guard their hearts and not get their feelings hurt and how to not over-react to something that happens or does not happen are in emotional and relational trouble. Some people leave a church because they got their feelings hurt. Some leave a marriage for the same reason. It's also called unresolved conflict. We can resolve anything short of death if we will just sit down with the person who hurt us and talk it out, expressing our real hurt feelings, but not blowing up, and not withdrawing from the person.

Tone of voice is paramount in communication. It's not what we are saying; it is how we are saying it. If we say something in anger, burning at the jets, we lose the other person. Exploding with anger drives people away. If we cool our jets, and talk about what hurt us with a calm tone of voice, we can get an audience, and better resolve the conflict. Unloading on others is not allowed, and no running off or stonewalling. We have to open up the sore spot and let the healing begin on us and the one who offended us.

I determined that I was not going to let anyone do anything to blow me out. It's not worth it. And it's not responsible, much less Christian. Jesus had His feelings in perfect control. He did drive out the money changers from the Temple, but that is "Righteous indignation," which is anger for a good cause. But He didn't throw stones at the guilty ones. Even when they spat on Him, mocked Him as being The Son of God, stripped Him of His garments and nailed Him to the cross, He maintained His cool, and forgave His tormentors and killers. Now that's self-control. It is not letting anyone blow you out.

We can get control of ourselves when we let God get control of us. His Holy Spirit produces love, joy, peace, patience, kindness, goodness, faithfulness, gentleness and self-control in us. But those are not raw human nature traits. That's why The Lord admonishes us to overcome our weak and easily offended flesh by His strong Spirit. All things are possible with Him. And it takes the spirit-controlled power of Him to keep our emotions in line with the word of God.

So the next time you are tempted to jump back at someone, either with words of anger or an all out attack of assault, or just running away because you can't control your emotions, remember Psalm 119:165. Stay at peace with God

yourself and others. Obey His Word. Make your hurt
feelings line up with the word of truth and you will be at
peace with whomever hurt you, and with yourself. It is well
worth the effort. Otherwise, anger builds up from
unresolved conflict, leading to depression, self-hurt and
isolation.

It's not what you're eating, but what's eating you!
The first time I heard that was in Christian Therapy in a unit
in Van Nuys, California. Nothing could be truer. When we
stuff our hurts and anger deep down inside us, and bury our
disappointments and emotional pain, from rejection or
failure or fear, we implode. The pressure of the stress will
break out somewhere. We hurt ourselves. I broke out in
gout, a swelling in the knees. The emotional pressure on the
inside of us from undue stress, and unresolved conflict,
could cause a heart attack. Stroke, some skin rash, or even
shingles.

Here's the formula. Meditate on the truth of God in
His word, and apply it to every situation we face in life.
God has the medicine to cure all ills. First, we have to be
informed before we can apply it to our needs. Everyone
needs self-control, and tons of it. Only God can give it to us
in a strong enough dose to get us under His control. We
then have peace, the peace that surpasses all understanding.
We have friends who stick closer than a brother. When we
get our feelings hurt, realize that feelings are not facts. The
word of God is facts. We can apply the facts and stabilize
our feelings and protect ourselves and others from more
hurt.

35

KNOW GOD BETER THAN OUR FAVORITE TV SHOW

W e can know God, personally. That is the best news I ever heard, and I heard it in college while reading a book in the library. The book was quoting John 17:3, where Jesus said, "This is eternal life, that we may know God through Him." From that point on, at age 19, I began to know God personally. I did it by reading the bible and renewing my mind on the truth about God, not what we hear on the street, or even in the church.

I became fascinated with God, especially after reading another book, *Mere Christianity*, by C.S. Lewis. I found out that Jesus is 'the' way to God. He came to earth to reveal God to us in person. He made claims that were unavoidable, that cried out for a definitive response. Boy, did I need direction in my life while in college trying to find the way to live, and what to do with my life. I found it. Eureka! Jesus is the way. No more searching for me. Now, fifty-one years later, I still find Jesus Christ to be more than enough. He is everything we need to connect with the

Father and Creator of this Universe and world. He gives specific direction to a wandering people on this earth, who are as lost as a goose in a snowstorm.

I discovered that Jesus is the way to self-control. We are all controlled by whatever we give ourselves to, whether it be drinking, giving in to sexual lust, sensationalism, money, success the world's way, accomplishments, or whatever we get attached to. Getting attached to The Lord is one safe life investment. He guides us into all truth and saves us from the lusts of the flesh, the temptations of the devil and the pressure of worldly people to conform.

We can know God as The God of love. He is love. Jesus perfectly demonstrated His Love on the cross for us. We desperately need love. God's kind of unconditional love. Human love is so conditional, as in, "I love you if you do whatever pleases me," and "I love you because you are so good-looking." How vain and short lived this is. We need longsuffering love, and it can only be found in our Father and His son. This kind of love will not let us go, no matter what we do. This kind waits on the prodigals to come back to the Father. This kind forgives us, and keeps on forgiving us, no matter what sin we commit.

When we know God we find out His Love for us sharpens our love for others. Otherwise, we give up on people. Heavenly love stays in there, forgives, restores, builds up and believes in people, even when they fail and run away from responsibility. The real sign of love is that it never gives up! It never quits! It always knows there is hope for everyone because it is longsuffering, not willing that anyone perish, or be cut off, even as God is.

We can know God as The Rewarded of those of us who diligently seek Him. Many people seem to think of

God as a punisher. That not true. He is called The Rewarded. We punish ourselves when we disobey or ignore God and His laws of righteousness. He rewards us when we obey and follow Him. He even forgives and restores us when we go astray. He will, however, allow us to learn the hard way, and that is how we often punish ourselves.

36

WHEN YOU ARE DOWN AND OUT

When you are feeling extremely low, don't know where to go, or what to do, do what King David did when he was in the Cave of Adullam, hiding from the Philistines behind enemy lines. David was thirsty for a drink of water from his own well in his own town. Thirty brave men risked their lives to go get him a drink from his well. When they got back with it, David poured it out as a thank you offering to God. It was too expensive to drink for himself.

David did something far better. He encouraged himself in the Lord. My goodness, how often do we all need to do that? We all get down and low in our feelings. We don't know what to do. We could become depressed or run away, or we could encourage ourselves in the Lord. After all, we are believers who are intimately connected with the Lord Jesus Christ, who make it through Calvary!

Think about His love, Think about His goodness, Think about His grace, which has brought us through thus far. For as high as the heaven's above, so great is the measure of our Father's love. Great is the measure of our Father's love. It will lift us higher than any circumstance can get us down.

Remember who we are! We are more than conquerors, through Him who conquered it all. He is able to keep us from falling into the deadly clutches of low esteem. He has already elevated us to the peak position of HIGHdentity. We are overcomers through His strength moving in us. We can make it with His help.

There is another way to encourage ourselves when we are down. That is, to put on the garment of praise for the spirit of heaviness. God implores us to in the 60th Chapter of Isaiah. The Lord has given us beauty for ashes, the oil of joy for mourning. He has turned our mourning into dancing. Now we can begin to praise Him, in spite of low feelings, bad circumstances and negative thoughts.

God inhabits the praise of His people. He gravitates to praise; so do we. Praise someone, really give them a compliment, and they will come close to you. When we praise The Lord, He literally comes into our presence. Praise attracts. Criticism repels. The same is true with God and man.

Praise is a choice we make in obedience to the Lord. He deserves praise. And He will make us praise in the earth when we praise Him. We praise Him for who He is the rewarder of our good attitude and words. We don't have to feel good to praise Him. But we can feel good about who He is, regardless of how we feel. When we release praise to Him, He flows through us with deep level encouragement.

Think up, even when you feel down. Sorrow may endure for a night, but joy comes in the morning. In the world we have many trials, but the Lord will bring us through them all. He wants us to trust Him while we are down and believe that He can lift us up. So we lift Him up by praising Him, and He will lift us up. We will be an encouragement to others, as well. Praise The Lord! He is worthy to be praised.

37

SIT - WALK - STAND

The most important step in walking with God on the level of HIGHdentity is being still and knowing that He is God. It involves sitting still, turning off everything else, and listening to the Father. There is a lot in the bible about 'waiting on God.' That doesn't mean to just sit and sleep or daydream. It means to bring every thought captive to obedience to Christ. First we must listen to God through His word in order to know how to think as He thinks. His ways are not our ways.

We must be Transformed....by renewing our minds on His truth. His wisdom transforms us from the flesh level to the spirit level. We begin to understand God and how we can operate on His level. But we have to listen to Him and tune in to Him to know His ways. We are what we think. But God is the master designer of thinking. He knows best.

The world's way is to walk in the counsel of the ungodly. People who don't know the Lord, and don't listen to His wisdom, do it their way. As the song went, "I did it my way." The problem is, as the bible states, "There is a way that seems right unto a man, but the ways thereof, are the ways of death." It further state, we are admonished to "Trust in the Lord with all our hearts, and lean not unto our own understanding."

Wise people fear God, and that is the beginning of wisdom. Ungodly people don't take time for God, and do it their own way. That's why our world is in such a mess. Ungodly men put the economy and worldly matters ahead of God. America has a spiritual problem. And it cannot be solved by money. It can only be solved by God, as He has revealed His Plan through Jesus Christ. And that is spiritual, on a far deeper level than the external effect of the economy. God gives eternal answers, not temporary ones.

After we sit and listen to God, we must walk in His light, and not stand with sinners. When we spend our time with sinners who are not repentant, we get caught in the vicious cycle of sin and death. When we follow Jesus who is the Light of the World, we increase in goodness, healthy relationships and personal well-being.

We must walk forward, not backward, always bringing up the past. Jesus knows the way. He is The Way. He is the Author and Finisher of our faith. He will get us to the finish line through the vicissitudes of life without our getting bogged down in problems. We can enjoy the journey, for He 'Endured the cross, for the joy set before Him.' Because he can do this, we can make it through anything we face and go through. God brings us to something to take us through it.

Then we must stand. We sit to listen, we walk to keep moving in God's purpose for us, then we stand on the truth, and not fall for the detours suggested by unwise men. We stand against evil, which is anything that draws us away from God. We stand for good, for all good comes from God. God is good, and all things work for good for those who follow God and His purpose for us.

38
STAY CONNECTED

So many people get cut off from the church and any accountable group and lose their edge on life. They go round and round in the same rut of thinking because they don't include anyone who would challenge their thinking. Life is not to be lived in isolation. God has called us into intimate fellowship with Himself, and His body, the church. This tells us why we need to stay plugged in to a church group.

Balance: We get out of balance when we get isolated out there by ourselves. We think the same way over and over. When we don't allow other's opinions, we become narrow and rigid. And that is not where real learning and growing occurs. We learn from each other. We don't have to agree with everything others say, nor do they have to agree with us. But we do need to hear each other out. We may have some wisdom that others need. They may be able to share a bit of wisdom with us.

Enthusiasm. Enthusiasm sharpens enthusiasm. People who isolate themselves usually get cold and bitter and unmotivated in life. Alternatively, when we gather with those who have a cause, like the cause of God through Christ Jesus to redeem the world from sin, we can stay enthusiastic. We need it. Otherwise, we burn out. Nobody has it in himself or herself to keep going strong on their own. God designed us to stay connected, to stay on fire with the purpose of helping each other make it through life with encouragement.

Direction: We all need direction from a good leader who follows The Lord. When we follow our own feelings we can get into trouble. But when we listen to proper guidance, we can stay away from getting hurt, and hurting other people. We desperately need direction. God provides it through pastors, evangelists, teachers, etc. Each has his or her own gift of leadership and can guide us all into a balanced, healthy, enthusiastic group of people.

Encouragement: We all need it. We all get down. We can help each other stay up when our feelings get low and our motivation is running out. Someone is always up, although we all get down at times. There is always someone who is up enough to encourage the rest of us to stay up and it works. Up produces up. Encouragement breeds encouragement.

39

SPIRITUAL STARVATION

I think the primary problem with us is that we are spiritually starved to death. We feed our flesh on all the things of this world, but don't take enough time to feed our spirits on the word of God. We are, therefore, weak Christians many times. We can't be strong in the Lord if we only feed our inner spirits on Sunday. We get drained before the first day of the week is over.

We have to be strong spiritually to overcome the obstacles and temptations and irritations of imperfect people on our lives. We must follow Jesus closely, keep our eyes on Him, or we will let the trials of life overwhelm us. He said, "In the world you will have tribulation. But be of good cheer. I have overcome the world." So can we when we remember what He said, and keep our focus on Him and His directing words of truth.

The enemy of our very souls will tempt us to settle for less than our best. To do things that detour us away from God's best for us. Jesus said, "Be perfect, as your heavenly Father is perfect." Now there is no way we can live sinless, due to our past sins. God forgives them. They are under the blood of Jesus. He expects us to stay away from sin, to lay aside every weight, and the sin that so easily besets us. He wants us to live free of hindrances to our maturity in Christ.

We can be perfect in our attitudes. We may be tempted to fail, but we can 'bring every thought captive to obedience to Christ.' He did it. He knows we can, also, when we stay close to Him. That's why He said, "Abide in me. Without me you can do nothing." He means we can do nothing productive in the kingdom of God. But, we can do all things through the Christ who died for us, redeemed us, and now lives in us through His strong spirit, to give us power to overcome anything that would bind us away from Him.

We must meditate on God's word day and night. The more we meditate, the more we take it into our inner spirits. , and the stronger we get in the Lord. For example, we can meditate on Psalm 119:165 and understand it. It is not practical to us until we think about it through constant meditation, until we immerse it in our spirits, and choose to apply it when someone hurts our feelings.

The verse in Psalms 119:165 says, "Great peace have we who love thy word, O God, and nothing shall offend us." I was offended by almost everything, until I learned to apply this truth. It works every time, but we have to first know it by heart, take it to heart, and protect our heart, the seat of our emotions, by obeying it on the spot. You can do it. I did it, and still apply it often. We need it. We must feed our spirits on it, or they will over-react.

40

CONFESS TO POSSESS

What we say is what we get! We have to confess to possess. In order to believe a truth enough for it to be a vital part of our lives, we have to say it, for when we say it, we re-enforce it in our lives. We tell our emotions what to believe. We must make our fickle feelings line up with the truth of God, or they will fall for whatever we feel in the natural world, and that can lead us into deep trouble and bondage.

Jesus simply said the word, and people were healed. We need to speak in faith, guided by the eternal word of God, and it will happen. The power of life and death are in the power of the tongue. We can literally think ourselves into living life more abundant. We have to believe it enough to say it out loud.

This is true even for salvation. When we 'confess with our mouths the Lord Jesus, and believe in our hearts that God has raised Him from the dead,' we are saved. Jesus said that if we confess Him publicly before men, He will confess us before the Father in heaven. What we really believe, we say.

We need to say, "I am More than a conqueror," even when we feel like failures. I did. It brought me from the pit of low esteem to the high place of HIGHdentity in Christ.

We say, "I am an overcomer." And we can overcome anything that binds us.

We say, "I can do all things through Christ who is my strength," and we can!

We say, "I have already passed from death into life by believing in Christ the Lord," and we have.

We say, "I always triumph in Jesus our Lord," and we can win every time.

We say, "I am the head, and not the tail," and we become what we say, the head!

We say, "I am for Christ Jesus," and we determine not to follow our feelings, only Him.

We say, "I am growing in grace," and we do, for we set the goal with our confessing and follow it through.

We say, "I am kind," and we become kind, instead of rude. It's that simple. We become what we say.

41

GOD USES A RESTLESS MAN OR WOMAN

There was a time in my life when I was so restless. I thought I was accomplishing little. My pace was slowed down and I wanted to see something productive happen. I got frustrated and left the slow pace, changed jobs, and got into a fast pace trucking job. I was really running from where God had me. I was used to doing active things with youth all the time, and I entered the pastorate and the pace was unbelievably slow, sitting in hospitals for long hours with parishioners.

While I was away from the slow pace and into the fast, I learned how restless I still was, even though I had changed. I wanted to serve the Lord, but had so much energy that I thought it was in the fast lane of hard physical labor and more active work. Boy, did I find out what life is all about. What I was really looking for was free worship. I was tired of tradition and the same rituals every Sunday, as a pastor. I needed fresh air.

I found it in a church that followed the Spirit, not just tradition. Jesus said, "The traditions of men make the word of God of no effect." How true. People get in a rut with the same thing. Jesus warned about vain repetitions. We can get up in the morning, for 30 days, and read the same chapter in the bible, and get too familiar with it. We do learn through repetition, but we need variety also.

I think tradition is like Psalm 46, "Be still and know that I am God." Whereas, contemporary is Psalm 47, "O Clap your hands, all you people. Shout unto God with a voice of triumph." Thank God for the tradition we grew up in. It taught us the bible and brought us to Jesus for salvation. As adults, we need to "Open up our hearts and rejoice before the Lord." Yes, that is being like little children. Jesus said we "Must become like little children to enter the kingdom of God."

We must learn to be teachable, free in expression and hungry for truth, like children. We need to allow creativity into our worship, or God may be bored with the same thing. When I was a youth minister in the 1970's, the leaders in the church made us stay in the basement on Saturday night with our creative worship. Now, most churches have realized that we must involve youth in worship every Sunday, or we lose them. Or they just sit in the balcony or on the back row, bored with the lack of creativity and involvement.

Part of being restless is not being satisfied with the status quo. David Wilkerson wrote a book called, *I'm Not Mad with God*, in the 1970's. It had a chapter entitled, "God Uses a Restless Man." The chapter really encouraged me to keep going and not give up on the system. People, systems and churches change when we see the need for change. We must first be open to the new.

The scripture encourages us to sing unto the Lord a 'new' song. We are in a 'new covenant with God. We are 'new' creations in Christ Jesus. God makes all things 'New!' We need to stay fresh and creative. Most of the world is so bored they resort to pornography and playboy style lusting, violence and crime for entertainment. God forbids we get that low.

It's time to stand up for decency and the sacredness of what men and women are supposed to share alone in the covenant of marriage, and the sanctity of every human life: no abortions. It's a child, not a choice. Perhaps the mother has lived fifteen to twenty years! How selfish to sacrifice the unborn child, who is a child in the eyes of God, for the mother who has had a chance at life and messed up by becoming pregnant out of wedlock. She and the father of the child need to repent. Let the child live, or they are guilty of murder of an innocent child.

We need to get restless about the perversion of sex in this land. Homosexuality is an abomination to God! That's the worst kind of sin. As mentioned before, it is totally backwards from what God planned by joining one man and one woman in Holy wedlock. Homosexuals can repent just like the rest of us. People aren't born to be homosexuals, as if they had no choice. There is always choice.

We are all born in sin and sin by our own choice. We all have to repent of sin and turn to Jesus for salvation, or we perish, which is unthinkable. Just because we are born in sin doesn't excuse sinning. God went to all the trouble to send His precious sinless Son into this world of lost people to save us. God forbids that anyone would justify sin, especially the president of the USA.

Thank God there are a few good men and women who are standing up for the values of our founding fathers, such as the republican candidates for president in 2012.

Most of them I have heard speak openly of having repented of sin in their lives and received Jesus as their personal Savior. They speak out about it, and how we need God in this country, according to one of them.

John Adams and James Madison said, "The constitution will only work for a moral and Judeo-Christian people." George Washington said, "It is impossible to rightly govern a people without the bible." We desperately need a president and other leaders who will stand for God's morality in the bible. We need those who will stand against the murder of unborn children, for any reason, and to stand against the perversion of homosexuality, and not compromise like so many of our present so-called leaders, who are cowards when it comes to standing for the truth of God.

I got tired of the status quo and being low and frustrated all the time. I started getting my mind renewed on the truth of God's word, and not falling into conformity with the world, or sometimes the church. I appeared before a bishop in the church in the 80's, who said, "It is dangerous to be led by the Holy Spirit." He was so status quo, like so many, that he was afraid to rock the boat with creative change.

I say, "It is dangerous to be led by tradition alone, with no openness to creative change, to meet the needs of the young people, and the older people, who want to grow up and be functional. If what we are doing isn't working, we need to change. The biggest change we need is to follow Jesus Christ, who is the Author and Finisher of our faith. God help those who stay conformed to the world, which is passing away. God help those who are here just to be entertained, and avoid worshiping and serving the Living

God."

It is high time for the church to come out of the shadows and go into all the world with the good news that Jesus Christ came into the world to save sinners, including all of us. Let the redeemed of the Lord, say so! Jesus is worth going to jail for, if they put us in jail for speaking of His name openly. That happened in the Book of Acts and it is happening in our own country. This country was founded with a cross at Cape Henry on Virginia Beach. Columbus planted a cross on every island he discovered. Let us take up the cross and follow Jesus in this once free land, not our fickle feelings, not ungodly leaders, not the vulgar entertainment industry. This country started out as a Judeo-Christian nation. Let's not lose it to the status-quo compromisers who don't stand for anything.

42

LET THE SPIRIT OF GOD PRODUCE FRUIT IN US

Human nature cannot produce the fruit of the kingdom of God. Only God can through His strong Spirit working in us. We are to receive His Spirit, according to Jesus, and be filled with Him, and follow Him into all truth. And He will produce good fruit in us. Else, we are enslaved to the bad fruit of our weak flesh.

The Spirit produces love in us, and displaces hatred, brought on by uncontrolled anger.

He produces joy in us, which is far superior to the temporary fun this world offers.

Peace flows like a river in us from the Prince of Peace, Jesus, and all strife has to go!

We begin to operate in patience because of the conviction of The Holy Spirit in us. Impatience is a thing of the past. We are becoming new creations through the power of God to change us flesh followers to spirit seekers.

Kindness drives out rudeness. Human nature can be so rude and harsh. The spirit of God changes it all into kindness. Kindness draws people to us and holds couples close together in marriage.

God is good, and only He can produce goodness in us. We are totally incapable without Him. Jesus said we can do nothing good without Him. With Him we can do all things good. He can radically change the 'bad to the bone' nature in us. Good goes deeper than bad.

God is faithful. He is longsuffering. He will not let us go. He is not willing that any should perish. We can become like Him as we walk with Him and allow His spirit to put the same faithfulness in us, otherwise, we are unfaithful.

The Holy Spirit is a gentleman. He is gentle. He can convict of sin, but always lets us decide to obey Him or not. We really need gentleness in our lives. Or we wear people down with our abrasive nature. God can sharpen that, and make us into loving people.

Self-control: We all really need more self-control. It is available through the power of God working in us by His Holy presence. We are out of control without God's strong and good control. God help us to have spirit-led self-control.

43

TILL WE ALL COME TO MATURITY IN CHRIST JESUS

Maturity to God is peaceful unity, being one in our Lord and Savior. We need to grow out of dissension and strife and unresolved conflict and buried anger and hurt feelings. When we get our feelings hurt, we need to apply the truth of Psalm 119:165, which says in effect, 'not to let anything blow us out, or make us come unglued.' Human nature gets offended and runs off. We need to face the music and stay in there and resolve whatever separates us.

God has resolved the eternal conflict between mankind and Himself through the blood of the cross. Sin is serious. It separates us from God. But He bridged the gap when He made peace between us and Him through the sacrifice of Jesus. That's taking the problem seriously, and doing something huge about it. Now that we have peace with God, as we receive His gift of reconciliation and forgiveness, we need to extend the same to those who offend us and hurt us.

We forgive by choice to obey God, for He says He will not forgive us our sins if we don't forgive others. That's heavy duty, but it cost God the earthly life and suffering on the cross of His son to pay the price in blood to cover our sinful nature and turn us back to God in righteous living. Even so, we can resolve any conflict between us and others who do us wrong or just hurt our feelings. We have to relay the forgiveness to them that God has given to all of us through Jesus.

Yet, forgiving others is not enough. We need to be reconciled to them, at peace with them, not hold grudges against them, no matter what they do to hurt us. Nobody will ever hurt us more than Jesus was hurt by our sins on the cross. He sweat drops of blood for us, and agonized about doing God's Will, against his own will, and going all the way to Calvary to save us from the consequences of our own sin. That is a huge price He paid to bring us back to Himself. He had to be just, so Jesus, The only just one, died for us, the unjust. Now we are justified by His pure blood.

The Book of Romans states that now that we are forgiven for our sins, we are reconciled to almighty God. We need to extend that blessing to those who offend us. We forgive them, and we allow them back into friendship with them, as if they never hurt us. Of course, it will take time to forget what they did to hurt us, but after we forgive, while it hurts out of obedience to God, then the process of healing will begin. Years later we won't feel the pain any more.

Think of it, God forgets our past through His very expensive sacrifice of His son. And He reinstates us into His forever family with no remembrance of our past. We need to do the same thing with others. Sometimes we forgive and still hold it against someone who wronged us. We desperately need to let it go, and let God heal us of our hurt and pain. Human nature can't do that alone. It is very vengeful. God makes it clear that revenge is His alone, not ours. He is the just judge, not us. Our responsibility is to forgive and start the process of forgetting, however painful it may be to our pride and hurt feelings.

We can't afford to let the sun go down on our anger. It will eat us alive, and ruin our relationship with God and others. We must cool our jets and let Christ be formed in us. He will give us the power to overcome our hot anger, before it consumes us!

To resolve conflict we need to not run away and hide from facing the truth. The imploders, those who keep conflict to themselves, and the exploders, those who let it out freely, need to meet together and resolve whatever is eating on them, and separating them. They must do it in the right tone of voice, not blasting, and not withdrawing. We have to be honest when our needs are not being met and we get hurt. But we need to express what our deepest needs are and allow another person to adjust to meeting them, though they have not met them in the past.

Giving another person another chance to meet our needs is very difficult for most people. We usually cut them off and run away, without giving them a chance to amend their behavior and gear to our needs. Everybody deserves a chance to do better. And we all usually do better when someone believes in us enough to give us an opportunity to do better. We all can change, and must adjust to meet each other's needs. We all have different expectations and emotional needs. But nobody is perfect in meeting them. We just need to be patient with people and allow them the decency of the right to adjust to us, and us to them.

44

BEING CONTENT WITH GOD

The biggest adjustment in life is learning to be content. Content in whatever state we find ourselves; whether we are in prison, like Paul, when he gave us this truth, or in sickness, when we don't feel good, or in separation from our loved ones for whatever reason, when we feel rejected, lose our job, or when we feel like failures.

We can be content with God alone, even when the bottom falls out in our lives, for God is willing and able to sustain us through the trials of lives. In fact, He says, "Many are the afflictions of the righteous, but The Lord delivers us from them all," Psalm 14. Of course, we will have many trials in this life, for God tests the righteous. We are not immune from trouble just because we are Christians or Jews.

Jesus said, "In the world you will have tribulation, but be of good cheer. I have overcome the world." How awesome is that? We just can't afford to put all our stock in this world, which is passing away. We need to put our faith and investment in the Kingdom of God, which is within us.

No matter what happens on the outside, we can be content to know God and have the eternal life of God's spirit flowing in us, to give us peace in the time of storm.

The Heavenly Forecast is, 'the meek will inherit the earth.' The meek are the ones of us with a teachable spirit, the ones who listen to the voice of the good shepherd, who follow Jesus Christ, not our feelings, conditioned by what is happening or not happening in this world. The meek humble ourselves before our God, and He will bring us through the troubles we face and go through.

The earth will be filled with the knowledge of the glory of God. That is a fact documented by the Old Testament prophets of God. The Lord is not limited to what is happening in this world which is evil. In fact, He will shake everything that can be shaken. Those who 'set Him always before us, will not be shaken.' For we are standing on solid rock, Jesus Christ, the only sure foundation. Praise God, and put your faith and investment in Him!

45

CONNECT AND CONTINUE

We can connect with God our Father creator through the blood covenant of Jesus Christ. God wants us back. Although we sin, and are sinners, God wants to convert us into saints, His own special people, who are righteous through the pure blood of the Savior. God has given us free status with Himself. We are righteous in His sight.

We need to get over our past and our low image of ourselves. It is true that we are just hot air without Jesus and the covenant connection He gives us with God. But God doesn't hold our past against us. As far as the East is from the West, so far has He removed our sins from us. We are sinless to God because of Jesus' sacrifice for us. We are redeemed by the perfect life sacrifice of The Lord.

No more labels for the people of God. Some ignorant pastor called me divorced after I had gone through that experience many years before. I would not stand for it. I am not divorced! I will not accept that label the rest of my life. My past is over. Almighty God doesn't hold it against me.

Neither will I allow anyone to put that label on me. I am a responsible Dad, who supported his three children all the way through college, and one through law school. I am still family with my three children and 6 grandchildren. Nothing is going to separate me from them.

Stay connected. Staying connected is what we have to do to maintain our HIGHdentity with the Lord God. Jesus has connected us in peace with our Holy Father, who does not permit sin. Now we are acceptable in His sight because of Jesus' great total offering of Himself for us. We are called out of darkness and ignorance and sin into the Light of God. Jesus is The Light of the World. No darkness, or evil, can get a strangle-hold on us. We are free to be our best, In Christ Jesus our Lord. He bought us with a very high price: His own blood.

To stay connected, we must continue in Jesus' Words. His Words are spirit and they are life. They give us hope when we sense no hope in the dying world around us. Continue means to always set the Lord before us. Because He is at our right hand, we will not be moved. God is shaking everything that can be shaken. Sinful, selfish, independent of God lifestyles will fall for they are built on the pride of man. Pride goes before a fall. The world system without God is doomed to fail.

Only those who put their faith in Jesus, the solid rock of our eternal salvation, will stand through the storms of life, and the judgment of God on sinful, unrepentant man. Our job is to stand, against evil, and lusts of the flesh, and lusts of the eyes, greed, self-righteousness and vain pride. We cannot afford to get entangled with any of those godless connections.

We need to invest in the kingdom of God, not the

world system. We can give to help those in need of food, housing and encouragement. A word fitly spoken is like a spark of life. We can lift up the fallen, the hurting, the lonely, the oppressed, by speaking deliverance and freedom in Jesus' Name. His name is above every name. He has the power to heal cancer, to drown out depression with impression of good and productivity.

We have the authority to do something about the problems overwhelming mankind. The answer is in the name of Jesus. He gives us the keys to the kingdom. Whatever we bind, will be bound. Whatever we loose, will be loosened. Meanwhile, we must stay intimately connected with Him, our power source, to release His blessing, healing and Salvation through our mouths to a world starving for hope.

As we stay connected with the body of Christ, the church, we give and receive the inspiration and challenge to go into all the world, and preach the gospel. Real preaching is effective when the Pastor delivers the truth to us, and we take it into all the world where we already are. We are laborers for Jesus. We are His ambassadors. It's up to us to get the truth out, that God is good, and all things work for good for those who love and follow Him.

Jesus gives us the final challenge saying, "as The Father has sent me, so send I you." The harvest is already white unto harvest. The harvest of souls is wide open. We need to take the bread of life to starving people. We can tell them how the Lord has saved us from sin and eternal loneliness and despair and frustration with ourselves. We need to regain the confidence of who we are In Christ: Overcomers, joint-heirs with the son of God.

We can develop the same mindset as Jesus. He came

to seek and save the lost. We need to get motivated to do the same. They don't necessarily come to us. We are to go to them. We have the spark in the good news of sins forgiven and a new life ready to be received. "To as many as received Him, to them gave He the power to become the sons and daughters of God." Let's take it to them. It's that good, and better when shared.

46

MARCHING TO ZION

I think of that old hymn my parents taught me in church. I think of it often. We really are marching to Zion, the beautiful city of God. My Dad's favorite song was, *In the Garden.* My Mother's favorite was, *When They Ring Those Golden Bells for You and Me.* I believe those old hymns really get us pointed in the right direction and give us eternal hope. They are worth repeating here.

I come to the garden alone
While the dew is still on the roses
And the voice I hear, falling on my ear
The Son of God discloses.
And, He walks with me, and He talks with me
And He tells me I am His own.
And the joy we share, as we tarry there
None other, has ever, known.
He speaks and the sound of His voice
Is so sweet, the birds hush their singing
And the melody, that He gave to me
Within my heart is ringing.

Think of those powerful truths I learned as a child.

God walks with us, and He talks with us, and He tells us we are His Own -- His own treasured possession. I think of our Grandson, Joseph Wilson Powell. He just had intestinal surgery, at three and a half months old. Just a little baby boy. Josh and Lisa, his parents, are right by his side all the time. That's the way God is with us. He is closer to us than breathing, and nearer than hands and feet. We just have to sense Him in our spirits.

We belong to God, not the world, or our sinful flesh nature or the devil. Jesus bought us back to be united with Him and the Father forever in heaven one day. Right now He is with us to guide us and lead us to the Promised Land. We can enjoy the journey with great joy in our hearts, no matter what is happening on the outside, God is on the inside with us, and will never leave us or forsake us. We are His, by His own choice and sacrifice to re-instate us back into His forever family.

Let us fear God. Not be afraid of Him, but concerned that we don't hurt Him by sinning and rebelling and living in the lusts and evil desires of this world. We are made for love, and to love. We are loved with an everlasting love, our Father's, through Jesus Christ our Lord. Let us exalt the name of Jesus above every name and march with Him, on to our eternal destiny.

The victory is already won! Jesus won it on the cross, for us, and all who believe in and follow Him. We are more than conquerors through His mighty Love. We can make it to the finish line. As our outward man wears out and gets older and finally dies, let us be sure to take the time to renew our inner man on the truth of God. And nothing can hold us back from being with our Lord forever. Amen, and praise the Lord forever!

47

LOVE SHARPENS LOVE

God's kind of unconditional, long-suffering, never giving up love always believes the best for other people, especially those who hurt us. It always responds positively to others, even when it is mistreated. Our human nature just can't come up with that caliber of love, but God releases it through us when we flow with Him.

Human love alters -- it is not consistent. God's love was expressed at the altar of the cross when Jesus gave His all for us. We need to stay at the altar of God, and our love for others won't alter. The Lord is consistent -- He is the same, yesterday, today and forever. We sure do need His kind of love. We can plug into it by laying hold of Jesus as He laid hold of us.

Love does not get into enemy territory, except to snatch the loveless out of the fire. The enemy wants us to hold grudges to hate, and to indulge in unforgiveness. On the other hand, God challenges us to love one another, as He loves us. It is impossible with our own human strength, but

His strength is made perfect in our weakness.

Love is not easily provoked. It can take it when it is hurt. It refuses to get offended. Human nature is easily offended, but The Lord fortifies us to hold our over-reaction and to allow His love to flow through us to those who need it so badly.

Love hardly even notices it when others do it wrong. Ha! Ha! That's a joke to human pride but not to the Author of Love. Jesus endured persecution, rejection, being spit on, mocked and crucified. He did it for us -- .fallen human beings, including the ones who nailed Him on the cross. What an example of forgiveness, as in, big time! He expects the same forgiving spirit from us.

Love will not withdraw or run away. It will respond positively to others, and certainly not ignore them. It stays in the connection when the going gets rough. It will not walk off, even from conflict. It sucks in its feelings and operates on the tender steel-like love of Jesus. That's when love sharpens Love, right when we want to take revenge or walk away in withdrawal. We can face the conflict head on. Love will cause the other person to cool his or her gears and get a grip on self-controlled love.

Love does not possess someone, but takes the leash off, and let's others be themselves. It doesn't have to be our way. We must allow others to be free to be themselves. They, in turn, will allow us to be ourselves, as well. We don't have to agree on everything. We can disagree agreeably. Our humility will draw us closer and closer. Possessing and demanding drives us farther apart.

Love agrees on the majors, that love, joy and peace are supreme. Because we receive God's unconditional love, we can give it to others, unconditionally. We don't demand anything, or try to force them to love us. We give love and then we get love. Giving produces getting.

Love endures everything. It will not quit. It loves people through their hard times. It believes the best for people, even when they can't see it for themselves. People really change for the good when someone believes in them, especially when they are down, and have a low concept of themselves. We need to feed people love. They are starved for it. It will feed their hungry souls and raise them up out of the pit of despair.

Love strikes the spark several times a day. It does not complain about the other person not being warm. It takes the initiative in reaching out to cold and hurting people who have been hurt badly by the lack of love. Love is patient and kind. It is amazing how simple it is. Just being kind to one another can re-spark the connection of love. And kindness produces kindness. It's very hard to be rude to someone who is being kind. God is kind. His loving kindness is better than life. So is ours when we extend it to others.

Sometimes the pathway of love is rough. There are obstacles in the way every day. True Godly love keeps on flowing around the hard places in life. It will not get bogged down in the whirlpools that would impede our loving each other. Love is tough. It won't stand still and avoid the hard places. It just keeps flowing on down the stream of life, with its focus on Jesus, the initiator of love that brings salvation to all.

48

AFRAID WE WILL TURN THEM OFF

I have heard so many people say, "I am afraid I will turn them off." The people I am speaking of are talking about sharing the gospel of Jesus with someone who may not be a Christian. My response is, "They are already turned off if they don't know Jesus!"

Some people erroneously think we should not impose our faith on other people. Answer: We can't impose anything on anyone they don't want to believe. People always have a choice. The people advertising lust, greed, selfishness, language and sexual out-of-control scenes are imposing their ungodly views and behavior on people who watch it -- I don't watch that garbage because I have a choice. When people complain about us imposing Christ on them, they need to know that His word clearly says that we are to "expose" them, and that is not imposing. If it's imposing on someone who is lost, as in the whole population on earth, to tell them about an eternal Savior who died on the cross for them, and everyone else, then they need exposing. Jesus said, "Go into all the world and preach the Gospel to every creature. Those who believe will be saved. Those who don't will be damned. And that's from the one who gave His life for our eternal salvation.

Here are some quotes from some people who need to be exposed:

"I don't have any love left for you!" I would say they don't know God's love which doesn't run out.

"Where was God when I prayed for you?" Answer: In the same place He was when Jesus died on the cross.

"Why did God let my child die?" Why did He let his only begotten, perfect son die? He did it for us and your child.

"God must hate me! He gave me an alcoholic or absent or controlling or non-affectionate or perfectionist father."

I believe people are responsible for their own behavior and their language. Alcoholics choose to take the first drink, when God warns us in His word in Proverbs, that strong drink is a mocker, a brawler, and he or she who is led astray by it is not wise. Plus, we are warned in 1 Corinthians 6:12 to not take unnecessary risks with anything that might enslave us. Our lives are our fault. No blaming.

Those whose dads were very imperfect are responsible to God themselves for their negative reactions to their dads. No dads are perfect. Evan an alcoholic or absent dad is no excuse for running away from a responsible life and not supporting your own kids, or using your dad as an excuse for bad behavior. There is a reason why many people are co-dependent on their parents' irresponsible behavior, but no one can use it for an excuse to do another wrong.

What if someone says, "It's too late?" Now, God never says that. He is not willing that anyone perish. But he is longsuffering with all of us. We need to do the same.

49

HOW FAR ARE WE GOING TO GO WITH JESUS?

Are we going to just accept His costly gift of salvation at the expense of Jesus' earthly life, and just sit down on our salvation on a padded pew?

Are we going to just go to church and not be the church in a dying world?

Will we just pray when we are down and out? What about praising God for who He is, not just what we can get from Him!

Are we going to just read the bible as permitted by the state literature, or be transformed by it?

Will we just love those who love us, or love unconditionally like Jesus?

Will we continue to allow abortion because many people see a child as just a choice, and murder him or her in the womb without a chance to breathe? God help us!

Do we agree with the world that homosexuality is an alternative lifestyle, when God calls it an abomination!

Will we get in the territory of addiction to alcohol by

taking a social drink?

Will we do anything harmful with our bodies when we are the temple of God?"

Do we vent our hot anger on those we love most, or will we not let the sun go down on our anger?

Do we give God and His church pocket change when He gives us eternal life?

Will we give God five minutes a day when He is available to us anytime?

Do we ignore or neglect so great a salvation, thinking, "I'm good?"

Do we think we are better than others, when God doesn't grade on the curve?

Will we spend most of our time being entertained by the world and its lusts when Jesus spent His short life being of total service to all mankind?

Jesus deserves our total commitment, meaning we need to renew our minds on His words daily and learn to bring every thought captive to obedience to Him. Plus, we need to make our fickle emotions line up with the self-control the bible challenges us to be in. We can be glad to dwell in the secret place of the most high God by meditating day and night on the word.

Follow Jesus. The one who came to this earth that we might have life more abundant. Really go after Him, as He came after us, and is coming again for us in His time. Lay hold of Him as He laid hold of us. Abide in Him. Stay close to Him. Let Him be formed in us. Share His love with everyone we come in contact with every day. He is worthy, of us, mind, soul and body. He bought us at the cross.

50

THE POWER OF AGREEING

I married a most lovely Western Lady, Patricia, just three months ago. She is attractive in every way. She is the best looking Grandmother I have seen. She is very affectionate and caring. She takes care of her aging Mother with tender care and understanding. She is repentant when she sins, which is rare. Most of all, she loves the Lord Jesus Christ with all her heart, soul and energy.

One very important thing Patricia has taught me is to pray right now. When one of our children or grandchildren has a need, we pray, together. She is constantly praying for our family and others who have great needs. Her strongest motivation is to get the truth of the gospel to people everywhere. That's the main point that attracted us to each other almost two years ago. We connected spiritually on the telephone, 3,170 miles apart, east to west. We kept building a strong spiritual relationship over the phone, and met for the first time in the Atlanta airport in May of 2011. We knew we were for each other when we met, for we were already connected deeply in spirit by the Lord.

The power of agreement flows strong in us. We pray that intimate connection for everyone. It is equally available to all, no matter what the past. The past is over. The new has come in Jesus. Patricia and I are reaping the benefit of much prayer and waiting on God to bring us together. When we met this year, we knew each other intimately, for the deepest connection is with The Lord and each other.

Jesus said, "When two or more agree on anything on earth, it shall be done." That's the power of agreement. Every couple can do it. It means dropping our pride, privacy and shame to pray out loud with each other. It's hard at first because it's really opening up our innermost soul to God and each other, but why not? We are each married to a person. Why not go all the way and develop the most intimate connection with each other, through the love, grace and spirit of our Lord.

We can do it. We can adjust to God's viewpoint and plan. All we have to do is hold hands and pray, and agree with the word of God. It will happen, in God's time. Yes, God has a waiting room, but it is filled with people of faith, who will not bow to the world and its temptations, especially on our time. We bow only to the name of Jesus Christ. Every knee will bow and every tongue confess that Jesus is Lord.

Get out the bible, dig into it and find out who you and your mate are in Christ Jesus. The more you find out, the stronger in the Lord you will be. I did it, going through a storm of very difficult years. God does allow us to go through the storms of life together. When we hold hands and hearts, we can walk through the dark with a spring in our step, a joy in our souls, and a smile on our faces. All of this is possible because Christ is in us, and is our hope of glory.

I think the glory has begun, and can begin for all of us who really abide in the Lord, together. The bible says that when we confess Jesus with our mouth, our whole household will be saved. Now that is exactly what we all need. Let us stand on the word and when we need healing, believe God heals, and confess healing by faith. We should further confess salvation for our loved ones and others who don't know the Lord yet. They will come in. Where else can they, or we, go, but to the Lord.

My grandmother told me as she was lying in a nursing home, paralyzed on one side, "The Lord is my shepherd." She was smiling with the joy of the Lord. My daddy lost both his legs during the last five years of his life here on earth. In spite of this tragedy he decided to get better and not bitter and he did. He made it through with the Lord. My mother had several strokes before she died. Even so, she was singing, "And He walks with me, and He talks with me, and He tells me I am His own, and the joy we share, as we tarry there. None other has ever known." Praise God! What a family of believers. I am forever grateful.

I love God, for He is our exceeding joy, our Father, who is a rewarder for those of us who diligently seek Him. I love Jesus, for He ransomed us from the curse of the law, and set us free from the consequences of our own sins. I love the Holy Spirit, for He fills us with the good fruit of God, and leads us into all truth. Blessed be the name of the Lord, both now and forevermore. Let us all praise Him, from generation to generation.

51

SNIFFING VERSUS TASTING

In the Book of Jeremiah the prophet of God warns the people of God about putting the branch to their nose, which being interpreted means, "Sniffing at God." God never allows lukewarmness in His people, whether it is Israel, His chosen people, the church, or the body of Christ.

God is for us. He is 100% committed to our eternal salvation. He sacrificed His only begotten son, Jesus, for our sins. He daily loads us with benefits, like health, food and shelter. Plus, He blesses us with every spiritual blessing in Christ Jesus. He will not withhold any good thing from those of us who love Him and follow His purpose. God is not willing for anyone to perish, or to be separated from Him in eternity. That is why He has given us eternal life in His son.

For us to take God lightly, especially the sacrifice of Jesus upon the cross is unthinkable. The bible warns, "How shall we escape, if we neglect so great a salvation," from the Book of Hebrews. Sniffing at God is neglecting the salvation He has given us at great cost. It's putting God on the back burner, and treating His blood covenant with us lightly.

God says He wants us to "Taste and see, that The Lord is good." Yes, taste, not sniff at. Many people are just looking, as the rich young ruler, who went away sorrowful because he had great possessions. He was not willing to pay the price of following Jesus, though it meant his eternal salvation to follow Him. Agrippa in the Book of Acts was 'almost persuaded.' He heard the testimony of Paul the Apostle after Paul was dramatically saved from a life of persecuting Christians. Agrippa was just playing with a strong testimony of the grace of God.

It's time for the church to wake up and get the message of God's awesome love to a lost humanity, but we can't do it if we are just sniffing at God. We must take up our cross, follow Jesus, go into all the world and preach the gospel before every creature. Those who believe will be saved. Those who don't believe will be damned. That is the word of God.

Awake oh church in America, put off your slumber, and the truth will set you free. For out of Zion comes your deliverer, in the year of jubilee. Oh, Hallelujah, Oh, Hallelujah, Hallelujah, praise the Lord. Let the people of God arise in this urgent hour. Let us get the message of the cross to a world perishing in 'self,' which is destructive to a vital relationship with God.

Self-indulgence is killing the people of the world. It sucks the life out of them. It mocks them. It gives them diminishing returns on the investment of their money and energy. Jesus challenges us to follow Him. This means self-denial, which is the far better way, since it leads to eternal life. Jesus made it clear the road to destruction, following the lusts of the flesh in the world, is broad, and many travel down it. Few go the narrow way of the cross to find eternal life.

Jesus set the example for God's will for our lives. He lived a life totally void of selfishness and worldly goods. He had one mission, to seek and save the lost. We get lost when we conform to the world instead of being transformed by renewing our minds on God's word. We are called out of the darkness of this world, which is controlled by Satan, a fallen angel. We are called into the marvelous light of God, which is lighted by the life and leading of Jesus the Christ.

When we taste and see that the Lord is good, we know that Jesus is worth every ounce of effort and energy we give to follow Him. His way is tough and challenging to our selfish nature, but it is totally satisfying to our souls. Once we experience God's wonderful grace, we will follow and seek His Face, not just His handouts.

Jesus is worthy of our total devotion, in mind, emotion, spirit and body. Once we get a taste of His Awesome Goodness, we will never go back to the hollow entertainment of the world, and its temporary lusts. Let us take up the cross and follow Jesus. Let us tell the world He is Lord and Savior of the world.

52

AWESOME REVERENCE

The bible makes it certain that God is more awesome than His holy places. We call people awesome and food awesome and cars awesome, etc., but God is not on that level. He is not just Awesome. He is more awesome than His very dwelling place. All of creation is very awesome in its beauty and design by the creator God. But God is even more.

He is more than His creation and the temples dedicated to Him, no matter how massive or ornate they may be. The difference is that God is extremely personal. He is much more than the expensive marble on the front of churches and synagogues. He is one with His son, Jesus the Christ, who plainly said He is. "One with the Father."

Now that is a huge revelation of The God of all creation. God is our heavenly Father. He is the one free spirit. He also has personal identity in being our Father. As an earthly father pities his children, so God pities and has mercy on His children, us. So much does He love us that He has paid the price to redeem us from the clutches of sin and death through the life, death and resurrection of Jesus.

We can be a personal part of God's forever family, in this life and in heaven when we die. Jesus came that we might have life more abundant. We have already passed from death into life by connecting with God the Father through Jesus the son. God lives in us through His holy spirit. He convicts us of sin, so we can repent and live God's way in righteousness, like Jesus. We all have that extreme potential.

First we must fear God, meaning we must stand in awesome reverence of Him as our creator God. We must dwell in His presence by meditating on His word, according to Psalm 91. After which we will abide under the shadow of the most high God, and be protected from any harm, for God will not let anything ultimately harm us, though He chastises, tests and tries us, to see if we truly love Him enough to obey Him.

Let the fear of God return to the church and to America and the whole world. How dare we take God for granted and not obey Him, and stand in awesome reverence of Him. He is worthy of all praise and honor and devotion and service. He bought us at the cross with the precious blood of Jesus. Let us fear Him by being totally committed to Him. Amen and Amen! Praise the Lord God!

53

BACK TO THE BIBLE

When I say something a little bit shady and off course, my wife says, "Back to the bible." By that she means for me to stay out of the gutter with my talk. How wise she is. Our whole culture needs to heed her advice.

When our libraries and schools and TV try to bring in Harry Potter as normal, I say, "Back to the bible." Harry Potter is witchcraft. God does not allow such in His kingdom. We need to turn off the TV when Potter is displayed in all of his gory stories. Our children deserve better than that, and so does God. He will punish all disobedience, just as He did with King Saul, who consulted a medium, who was into witchcraft. God is the authority and so is Jesus. Witches and blood splashers are not the authority.

Halloween is an over-accepted pagan holiday in our country. People bring in their kids by the pick-up truck loads to get candy. This much is acceptable, but to dress our little ones up in witch costumes and skull outfits and bring on the spirit of fear with haunted houses and devil-honoring attire is too much. We need to have Hallelujah Parties on Halloween, just as one of my churches did in Tifton, Ga. Everything is geared to Adam and Eve and other biblical characters. They serve heavenly hash, not devil's food cake.

Jesus conquered fear, especially the fear of death which hangs over the entire human race. He did it by reversing the curse of human sin that brings on the punishment of death, which is separation from God now and in eternal Hell. No Fear with Jesus. He said, "Fear Not!" Because He lives, we can face tomorrow, with no sorrow. We can face almighty God without shame and disgrace and condemnation because Jesus is able to keep us from falling, back into sin and shame, and to present us faultless before His presence with exceeding joy.

Satan is no joke. He is a fallen angel who has the limited power to tempt us to sin and disobey God. He comes to kill, steal and destroy. He is the father of lies, and operates on deception, as when he deceived Adam and Eve into eating of the fruit forbidden by God. Satan lied to our first parents. He said, "You will not truly die if you eat the forbidden fruit." Adam and Eve bought the lie, ate the fruit and died spiritually. Thereafter, the curse of sin and death hung over this earth until Jesus came and reversed the curse and blessed us with forgiveness of our sins when we repent and overcome sin, by the power of God's spirit working in us.

We have authority over Satan. Jesus extended His authority to us. He has all authority in heaven and on earth. We dare not bow to a rebellious angel who fell like lightening out of heaven itself. Jesus made it clear that our love for Him is shown by obedience, as in keeping his laws in the Ten Commandments. The government and not-so-supreme court took the Ten Commandments and prayer out of our schools and all hell broke out, with armed robbery, terroristic threats, killing, rape and rebellion against God.

Our ungodly so-called leaders put God on the back burner, or in the margin of life, as does Obama the compromiser. We now have a weak coward in the White House who will not even stand up for an unborn child. Even worse, he endorses homosexuality as an alternative lifestyle, even approving it in the marriage of two homosexuals. God loves homosexuals, just as He does other sinners. He calls the sin homosexuality an "Abomination!" Such behavior brings on the judgment of God, as in Sodom and Gomorrah, when God rained down fire and brimstone on the people involved in the perverted lifestyle.

Back to the bible. Hollywood needs to heed my wife's advice, too. They show the young girls and even older women, half dressed, exposing their almost naked bodies to the public, tempting people to lust, for man is turned on by sight. Jesus clarified that when a man looks with lust after a woman, he is guilty of lust. Lust leads to the death of love, because it makes animals out of people. Women, too, lust after men and their bare chests and lustful moves, as demonstrated by Michael Jackson. What a disgrace. Our children deserve better, and can have better when they follow Jesus, who walked in love, not lust.

Playboy promotes lust, fornication and adultery. God must cringe at their perversion. When a man and woman are meeting each other's needs in marriage, they dare not look at the latest centerfold. It should be labeled, 'sinner-fold.' I don't want lust to water down my love for my wife. I will and do give her all my affection and love and care and adore and cherish her. All of these lustful groups need to do it God's way, as in back to the bible. Sexual desire and function, out of the context of marriage, is sin. God forbid that we should allow our children to watch the very sinful, lustful behavior of Hollywood and movies and TV and others who pervert God's intention for a man and a woman.

We desperately need to get back to the bible. George Washington believed that it is impossible to rightly govern a people without the bible. How right on he was. John Adams and James Madison pointed out that the constitution works only for a moral and biblical people. Edmund Burke emphasized that the less self-control we put on our own lives, the more the law enforcement authorities have to put us under their control.

The only place we can find real self-control is in the bible, God's book of right living, as demonstrated by Jesus the Christ. It is not really self-control, it is spirit-control, instigated by the spirit of the living God living in us, and giving us the power to control what our eyes see, what we feel in our emotions and what we do because of what we see and feel. We can learn to operate in obedience to God's word, and not give in to the lusts of the world, which deplete our money and energy and never satisfy the deep longings of our hearts.

I am forever grateful to say that I have found life more abundant by following the Savior and Lord of The World, Jesus, The Righteous, who leads us into all truth, which sets us free to be our best selves. Thank God for a perfect example in Christ of what life can be. His lifestyle is potentially ours, for we can do all things through Christ Jesus our deep inner strength. He gives us His unconditional, self-controlling love that saves us from the limitations and self-destruction of the world's cheap human love.

Back to the Bible. It is the source of all truth. It has the backing of almighty God and our Lord and Savior Jesus Christ. It works. And we can know and follow it as we follow the one who bought us at Calvary at a great price. We belong to Him. Let's get back to God and His bible.

54

I ANITCIPATE MY MATE

I love my wife with all my heart. I show it with my actions. I meet her at the door and greet her with a kiss and we hug each other with all our might. I can hardly wait to arrive at home from work in time to meet her for lunch as she comes in from keeping her mother. I am as glad to see her as she is to see me.

We eat lunch together and enjoy the time around a warm fire. I like to cook for Patricia. It gives me a sense of doing something important for her by surprising her with a creative meal. Then we go back to work, me to the library to type my manuscript for this book I am writing, and she back to her mothers' house to take care of her loved one.

We meet after work in the late afternoon. It is almost dark at 4:30pm out here in Washington State. We enjoy supper together and then relax and watch TBN or Daystar TV, which is filled with good and encouraging Christian teaching, preaching and singing. It is so easy to keep our faith built up on the word of God, listening to Joseph Prince, Joel Osteen, T.D. Jakes, and John Hagee. The 700 Club and

TBN really have people broadcasting who are into Jesus, as He is in them, building up the body of Christ.

Patti and I also read the bible together at noon and at night when we go to bed. We pray the word of God, and stand on it. We pray for our children and grandchildren several times a day. We have experienced the power of two people being united in Christ, to pray and stand in the gap for our families and our country. Jesus directed us in prayer by teaching, "Where two or more agree in prayer, it shall be done." We encourage couples everywhere to join together in prayer, and be united on the deep, spiritual level with God and each other.

The greatest thing about marriage and holy wedlock is that we are united in spirit, empowered by the Holy Spirit Himself, the very personal presence of God our Father. In The name of Jesus we are praying in line with the will of God. He will release His power through those of us who agree in prayer together and pray for the salvation and healing and deliverance of people. Let us all pray often, "Not my will, but Thine be done, O Lord," as Jesus prayed in the garden.

We dance together. Dancing can unite us in a very personal and emotional way that nothing else can. The music is very motivating and romantic and gives us a lift in our most important relationship. I used to go to dances in Savannah, Georgia. Now my wife and I have our own dancing and drawing us closer and closer together in the bond of intimacy.

Holding hands can be such a lift and a bonding between husband and wife. We need to touch much and stay close to the ones we love most. There is power of intimacy in holding hands and keeping our hearts in tune with each other. Rubbing each other's back is also very bonding. It relaxes us and feels good and makes us feel closer than we have ever been before.

Patti and I tell each other, "I love you" throughout the day. We text each other very often and remind each other of our commitment to stay in love. It's really easy, and enjoyable. The key is in reciprocating love, not just receiving it, or just giving it out. Love does produce love. When one reaches out and touches the other one, the spark is rekindled, causing the spark to grow into a flame of love and caring about each other's deepest needs for affection, and lots of it. Can we ever get enough? No way.

I like to put Patti's shoes on for her as she gets ready to go out in the morning, or out after lunch. We do take our shoes off when entering the front door of our house. Patti has the sign up to remind us. It not only saves our carpet and floors, it relaxes our feet, which can be pretty tired after a hard day's work. We massage each other's feet with oil and Japanese body butter. It really feels enervating and it rejuvenates our tired feet.

I especially like to surprise Patti with homemade soup or my own version of Spanish rice. It usually includes everything left in the fridge, and almost the kitchen sink. Patti surprises me, too. She does nice things for me like grabbing me from behind and hugging me with a bear hug. I like that very much.

Intimacy in marriage is very easy. It just takes time to slow down and not be in a hurry, or too busy, or too tired. It's the little things we do for each other that trigger romance and the spark of love. We think we can stay in love, just by doing the little things that make a relationship so close and intimate. Just noticing each other and giving our undivided attention to our mate can revolutionize our marriages.

My prayer is that the Hollywood stars and the Playboy people and the divorce court demanders would get a high view of marriage and not flaunt their lustful bodies and empty souls on the screen before all of us, including our children and teens, and set a good example of healthy marriages and relationships. We desperately need good examples of Godly relationships in marriage and single living, where people respect each other's privacy and regard sexual activity as sacred in the holy wedlock of marriage.

One of the leaders in marriage counseling stated that, "People don't change much after marriage." This may be true in the sense that we all form patterns early in childhood, but it is not true in the sense that we must all constantly change. All kinds of relationships in life require change and adjustment and self-denial to make them work effectively. Strife comes out of selfishness and unwillingness to adjust. We actually do adjust or bust. Too many bust up a marriage with divorce. Let that be in the past! God forgive us, and restore us to good relationships, with the man leading by meeting needs, and not dominating and demanding submission from the woman.

The woman can meet the needs of her husband by understanding the differences between men and women, such as women are 'feelers,' primarily, while men are 'Fixers,' primarily. I overheard a lady say in a store a few years ago, "Do you know what my husband was thinking when I had an emotional moment?" I couldn't wait to hear her answer. She said, "He was thinking, did I change the oil in my car?" What a good description of male-female differences.

When a woman has an emotional moment, a man

either watches football or goes to sleep. Why? We are not being cruel. We just grow up learning to play football, to be tough and not to cry. We don't know how to handle emotional moments, until we wise up, after our wives cool down with their anger because we are unschooled in that area. Give us a break to learn to be comforting and understanding. We can do it men, but we have to listen to our women, and study their emotional makeup, by bending our male pride and distance to be close to them when they need us most.

I anticipate just about everything Patti and I do, even just being together and relaxing and affirming each other, listening to each other (we all need to ventilate our stress of the day, and our celebrations). Most of all, we need to be less sensitive when our mates say something that might grind on our feelings. We need to, above all, guard our hearts, for out of them are the issues of life. Whatever scratches our hearts scratches us. We just have to learn to tone it down and not do heart surgery on minor scrapes.

Build each other up. We can do it. We can constantly compliment each other and remind each other who we are in Christ. This will seal off all hurt feelings from erupting into a volcano of runny emotions. We are more than conquerors through the grace and love of Jesus. We need to make our feelings line up with such truth, and live by every word of God, not by our hurt feelings and sensitive emotions.

We need to remind each other that we both can overcome anything that separates us. Even unfaithfulness can be forgiven, if the guilty one is repentant. The hurt one forgives according to how God has forgiven us all, through the sacrifice of Jesus on the cross. We can never forgive if we focus on our hurts and emotions. We need to grow up into maturity in Christ and forgive as He did from the cross to His accusers and those who put Him up there!

We can do it. We can repent quickly of anything or of any hurt that would separate us from the one we love the most. We can be forgiving, instantly, as Jesus was. We can get over past hurts if we nail them to the cross, and allow the Lord of Glory to heal us of being rejected and hurt by the things we do or don't do that irritate our weak human flesh. Let us put on the garment of praise to God for giving us the perfect example of love and peace and forgiveness in Jesus. Let us drop forever the spirit of heaviness that comes from an unforgiving heart and an emotional cavity filled with unresolved conflict.

55

GET A GRIP ON OUR GREAT GOD

If you are bored with God I don't think you have met the Father of our Lord Jesus Christ!

Are you lonely? He will never leave you or forsake you. His presence is spiritual and closer than breathing and nearer than hands and feet.

Are you depressed? Jesus will impress you to life, for He made it through the wilderness of personal temptation by the devil, through the garden of standing alone on the eve of His death, through Calvary, dying for those who crucified Him, and all of us sinners on this planet.

Are you in debt? He paid a debt He didn't owe; we owed a debt we couldn't pay. We all needed someone to wash our sins away (that's the sin debt!) Jesus actually bought us back from the terrible consequences of our own sinfulness, at the cost of His own pure blood! The debt is paid. We are given eternal life. We can now connect with God the Father through the son and know the Creator of the Universe, of each of us, and live in intimate fellowship with Him forever and ever.

Do you feel unloved, or rejected by those around you? We are loved, with an everlasting love of the Father. It is uniquely unconditional, longsuffering and totally supportive.

Are you stressed out? Cast all your cares on Him, for He cares for you. He will sustain us through whatever we have to plow through in this life.

Are you Sick? He is the healer of all mankind. By Jesus' stripes we are healed! He sent His word and healed us through blood. We can speak the word of healing and give hope to hurting people who are in a state of disease.

Are you lost? Have you lost your way? Jesus is mighty to save. He is the Savior of mankind. He is not willing for even one person to perish. He had rather die than live without us in eternity. Be found today.

We can get a firm grip on our great God. The answer is found in a song of the 1970's, *Day By Day*:

To See Thee more clearly!
To do that we must behold His Glory in the Word of God every day. And then we can reflect His Glory.
It's not us; it's Jesus through us, shining like the Light of the World that He is.
To Love Thee More Dearly!

Greater love has no man than Jesus' love when He lay down His life for us. We are too selfish to love God in our flesh, but we can respond to His love. He loved us first. We can love Him back. We can share His love with people who have not met Him and don't know His love yet. The greatest love we can give is to encourage hurting people when they are down. We can encourage and comfort them because we have been encouraged and comforted on the deepest level by Jesus Christ. He believes in us. We have the privilege of believing in others and giving them a word of lift, to boost them out of their hole they are in because life didn't go their way. Life works God's way. Let's share it.

To Follow Him More Nearly. To stay close to God by dwelling in His secret place through prayer and meditation on His truth. We will get so close to Him we are literally transformed. We can set our affections above, where God and Jesus are, and we will live above the vicissitudes of life in the valleys of stress and defeat here. Yes, we can follow Jesus more nearly as we keep our eyes on Him, not the world that is self-destructing. Let us lay aside every weight, and the sin that so easily besets us, and lay hold of Jesus, as He laid hold of us on the cross.

God is good. All things work for good as we follow His purpose. Get a grip.

God is our exceeding Joy. There is no sorrow that His presence cannot heal with the Joy of knowing it will get better, and we can endure anything because of His love and Presence with us, and in us.

God is a rewarder of we who diligently seek Him. Let us press on into Him and His word and we will be rewarded with great joy, peace and love for all. Get a stronger grip on Him. He is solid rock

56

PARDON ME BOYS,
IS THIS THE ICE CREAM TRUCK TO
WALMART?

I was extremely amused recently when my four-year old granddaughter said she wanted to ride the ice cream truck to Wal-Mart. Wow! What a thought for a child. Sounds a lot like our human flesh crying out to be gratified with the delights of this world. Even Billy Graham still likes ice cream; so do I. I will have to inform Stella Rae there is something a little bit richer and higher than ice cream. It's called the bread of life.

Jesus said, "I am the bread of life. Whoever comes to me for food will never be hungry again." What a profound promise. Jesus has really made some astounding claims about Himself. This one has to do with the deep satisfaction we long for in our very souls, not just our bodily appetites for ice cream.

Pascal, the great Physicist of the 17th Century, made a penetrating remark that has stuck with me over the years. He said, "There is a God-shaped vacuum in each of us that can only be filled by God, as He is revealed in Jesus Christ." Now that's a loaded potato statement. We all ride the ice cream trucks of life, trying to be filled with material things which just don't penetrate to the depths of our souls. How much ice cream can we eat?

The truth is that Jesus gives us living water to quench our thirst for eternal life and God. It can flow in us, through us and out of us, bubbling up into an eternal spring of thirst-quenching water. It is what satisfies our souls, because it fills the vacuum created by sin and lust in our lives. Only God can fill us to overflowing. He does it through Jesus and His holy spirit flowing into us with eternal life.

57

SELF-HELP WINDS DOWN TO ZERO

I've heard several people say they want to go out in the world and find themselves. That is very interesting. Hollywood is a good example of people trying to find themselves, in glamour, show biz, self-indulgence. Lust for money and sex, and self-indulgence. The results from the screen city are not good at all. Somebody is always leaving someone else, or cheating on them, or just failing to match up, not to mention the illegitimacy rate with multiple partners.

Our world is saturated with people who are trying desperately to find themselves in the rat race to the top. The problem being the top turns out to be the bottom of fulfillment, because fulfillment is never found in self and self-indulgence. Human lust for money, sex and things is never satisfied. These things can never satisfy us because we are made for God, and only He can satisfy our inner souls.

Jesus made it clear that we who would like to find life His way, as in eternal life, must deny ourselves the lusts of this world. Take up our cross, as in, cross out the big "I," and follow Him. He is about service to others, not about self. He always denied Himself. In fact, He humbled Himself, and stepped down from heaven with the Father God, and took on weak and limited human nature, just like us. What a huge step away from the completeness, harmony and peacefulness of heaven.

To follow the Lord means God first, others second, and ourselves last. It worked for Jesus. He did the will of God, to seek and save the lost. Our goal needs to reach people who are cut off from the Lord in sin with the hope of eternal redemption. No, we don't have to be afraid of turning them off. They are already turned off, without God. We could help to get them in position to be turned on to God, His promise of life more abundant, peace, love, joy, forgiveness and Self-Control.

The rich young ruler who came running to Jesus to find out how to get eternal life was so enshrouded with wealth and things of this world that he turned down eternal life for temporary riches. What a loss. What does it profit a person to gain the whole world and lose his or her own soul? It is unthinkable, but choosing Jesus and self-denial is the way to find our true selves in oneness with the son of God, and be utterly fulfilled.

58

TAKE THE SPURS OFF

If there is one thing we need to do to stay in healthy relationships and marriage, we need to take the spurs off. We need to drop the charges we bring against each other when one of us says something to offend us and we get our feelings hurt.

We can practice the principle of not getting offended, as found in Psalms 119:165. We must guard our feelings against being easily provoked. Love God's way is not easily provoked. Human nature is easily provoked. We can guard against being set off in our emotions so easily by keeping a guard over our feelings.

Couples spur each other over little things that really don't matter. It all comes down to selfishness. We all want our own way, and when someone chooses another way, we let it drive us up the wall. We must learn to take the spurs off and not unload our anger over things that could drive us apart, unless we resolve them in calmness and agreement.

Bringing up the past is spurring. We need to learn to forget the past hurts and wounds, by not tearing them open again. When we forgive, we forget. It may take a long time, but we must refuse to hold something against someone by bringing it up, after we have forgiven them. We don't really forget past hurts, we just defuse them, and refuse to let them eat on us.

We need to put on the gentle spirit of affection and friendly connection with our mates. If they hurt our pride, we can assuage it by choosing not to overreact in anger. Instead, we could do something nice for them, like giving them a massage with a gentle touch of love and compassion.

My wife actually does that for me. We both turned away from each other after a disagreement. It was getting icy cold between us. Withdrawal had neutralized our relationship until she reached across the cool chasm between us and rubbed my back with icy hot salve. It wasn't so much the salve as it was her gentle touch that broke the ice between us.

We can stay close, when we don't let disagreement and argument drive us into the icy waters of distance. We have to resolve it rapidly with a move to get close again. Feelings are the direct result of what we do to build relationships. We must act, or we freeze out a good relationship. Good produces good. Warmth produces warmth. Love sharpens love.

59

REPENT QUICKLY

When we do something wrong, we need to repent quickly. We must really mean it from our hearts, for Godly sorrow leads to repentance. Sorrow alone is not enough, like being sad we got caught, or convicted by God's spirit that we did something wrong. We need to really turn away from whatever we did amiss and turn to the God who has redeemed us through the blood of Jesus Christ. He paid a heavy price for us, so let us not disgrace Him by taking our sin against Him lightly.

We also need to repent quickly when we hurt someone, especially someone we love, which means we need to apologize immediately. We need to not allow a hard heart to set into us as we harbor anger or resentment for someone. When someone else hurts us, we need to forgive right away, and not wait for the icy cold grip of distance to keep us away from the person.

The worst thing that can happen is for bitterness to take root in us because we bury our anger and don't release it in a positive way, as in a clear expression of our hurt, but not unloading it on someone else. When we let anger build up inside us, it can get a strong grip on us called a stronghold. Strongholds are difficult to break. It is much easier to prevent the strong grip of anger leading to bitterness inside us by dealing with the conflict on the spot.

We can stay clear of all wrong and anger and bitterness when we stay close to God through His mighty convicting word. As we read His truth, all lies, anger, bitterness, resentment and grudges must go. We then become free to love others without resenting them. God will bless us with His peace that passes all understanding.

60

IS THIS THE SLIM-FAST BUS TO THE GYM?

Seems like that would be a bit more mature than the ice cream truck to Wal-Mart. Better still is the slow-boat to God's waiting room. It is there we will learn to deny ourselves all the surface pleasures of this life by digging into the deeper meaning of our existence down here on earth, which can become real living instead of just getting by or existing.

We live in a microwave society where we can pop anything edible in the quick oven and get instant results. But living in fellowship with our Heavenly Father is not so fast! We have to stand in the gap of faith to really build our trust in God. And we must trust Him with the results, and not demand that He give us rapid results.

It seems that God wants to know if we are willing to live from the inside out, instead of the outside in. We are not here to just be entertained, though more of us like movies and sports. We are here to develop patience and endurance as we learn to trust God in life, especially when nothing explosive is happening in our lives.

In God's waiting room we learn that His strength is made perfect in our weakness, and that His grace is sufficient for every need we have, in particular our need to be patient with each other, and with God. The Lord wants us to prosper and be in good health even as our souls prosper. The ten lepers who were healed weren't even grateful enough to turn around and say thank you to Jesus for healing them, except for one. They prospered in body, but not in spirit. This is the main thing God wants us to do - -to cultivate the inner spirit in us, not just the outer shell.

One thief on the cross was patient enough to wait for Jesus to remember Him when He came into His kingdom. Jesus assured him he would be with the Lord this day in paradise. The impatient one who wanted down off the cross right away, lost in both worlds.

61

JESUS COME

Jesus Come, and meet us here
We want to know Your Love again
Jesus Come, and be our Lord
And make us in one accord!
Fill us with Your Love
Touch us with Your Power
Let Your Spirit come right now
We are waiting, just for You.

Jesus Come -- and be formed in us -- that we might live in peace -- as you are our Prince of Peace.

Jesus Come -- and be our Wonderful Counselor that You are -- for we need Your wisdom from on high.

Jesus Come -- for You alone are our All in All. You meet every need we ever had or will have.

Jesus Come -- for we are weak in our flesh -- and we need Your mighty strength in our weakness.

Jesus Come -- for you give us eternal life -- lest we perish without You.

Jesus Come -- and fill us with Your love, for our human love is all too thin to hold us together.

Jesus Come -- for You alone are the resurrection and the life. Without You we are but dust in a museum.

Jesus Come -- for down here we have nothing of lasting value, but in You we have everlasting life.

Jesus Come -- and still our souls, that we not strive away our energy in conflict with our neighbors.

Jesus Come -- free us from the chains that bind our souls and set us free to serve You.

Jesus Come -- and fill us with Your strong holy spirit, for we are but flesh without You.

Jesus Come -- and set us on fire with Your love so You might love some lonely soul through us.

Jesus Come -- we are waiting, just for You, because You alone can give us life more abundant.

Jesus Come, and be our Lord
We want to live in one accord!
Jesus Come, and set us free
To be the best we can be!
Fill us with Your love
Touch us with Your power
Let Your spirit come this hour
We are waiting, just, for You!

The above poem is my prayer daily. I pray that Christ will be formed in us. Let us draw near to Him in meditation and in prayer and stay close to the only one who can lift us above the storms in life. As the eagle soars above the clouds of rain, so we can soar above the trials that would offset us and detract us from keeping our eyes on The Master of Eternal Life.

Jesus is the chief cornerstone. He is a tried stone, a

sure foundation, the solid rock of our eternal salvation. We need Him to give us the advantage over all the temptations and trials in life. He mastered every conflict He encountered, and overcame this temporary world and its allurements. We can overcome this world also as we focus within on the Kingdom of God, which is Christ in us, our hope of glory.

Jesus is the Wonderful, Counselor, The Mighty God, the Everlasting Father. He is the Prince of Peace. This world desperately needs Him for the wisdom to live a fulfilling life. We need His power to be able to deal with all the problems in life. We need His peace to live in harmony with those around us every day, especially those we are closest to and love in our families.

Till by faith I met Him face to face, and I felt the wonder of His grace, then I knew He was more than just a God who didn't care, who lived away up there, and now He walks beside me day by day, helping me to find the narrow way.

Biography

John W. Powell was born to and raised by his wonderful Christian parents, J.W. and Stella Powell. He graduated from Georgia Southern University, Emory University Theology School, and Logos Christian Graduate School in Jacksonville, Florida.

Dr. Powell enjoyed youth ministry and being a pastor in the Methodist Church for twenty-five years. He really connected with prisoners in prison for eighteen years, and taught them the truths in this book.

He recently married Patricia Ann Pfeiffer of Lacey, Washington, where they reside, and enjoy an awesome marriage together. Patricia is a wonderful match for John, as he is for her. They also have a home in Claxton, Georgia, where they plan to live during the winters.

www.ingramcontent.com/pod-product-compliance
Lightning Source LLC
Chambersburg PA
CBHW031318040426
42443CB00005B/118